The Silver Pearl
Our Generation's Search for Meaning

JIMMY LAURA SMULL, PH.D. AND CAROL ORSBORN, PH.D.

AMP&RSAND, INC.
Chicago, Illinois

First Edition – 2005
Second Edition – 2007
ISBN 978-0-9761235-3-8
Book Design: David Robson, Robson Design
Cover Art: Guy Billout
Cover Art Coordinator: Tom Moyer, M1 partnership
Author Photos: Figge Photography
Published by Ampersand, Inc., Chicago, Illinois
Printed in the United States of America

AUTHORS' NOTE

Participants in the research study and in the Silver Pearl Network Workshops and Retreats have contributed case histories, wisdom and anecdotal support for the principles shared in this book. When requested, we have honored their desire for anonymity by changing personal names and fictionalizing details. Unless otherwise indicated, traditional stories shared in this book including The Legend of The Silver Pearl have come from multiple verbal and written sources and have been adapted for our purposes.

Some of the authors' material has been derived from *Healing Eve, The Art of Resilience, Speak the Language of Healing* and *Nothing Left Unsaid.*

Finally, we wish to extend our deepest gratitude to our publisher, mentor and muse, Suzanne T. Isaacs.

DEDICATION

*To the generations of women who came before
and the gift of their pearls*

TABLE OF CONTENTS

CREATING A LEGACY

MEANING

APPENDIX

ACKNOWLEDGEMENTS

To my Aunt Lois, who loved me unconditionally, and by example, taught me how to take the journey to wisdom.

To my family: soul mate, Les; son, Jack; stepdaughter, Lauren; and stepdaughter, Kerri, whose love has paved my way to the silver pearl.

And finally, a special thank you to my co-researcher, co-author, and kindred spirit, Carol Orsborn. Being able to collaborate with you on this book is my reward.

JIMMY LAURA SMULL, PH.D.

With deep affection to Dorothy Orsborn, *Mom O*, for gifting me with my first and favorite silver pearls. Great Spirit, grant us many more miles together in each other's moccasins.

To Leean Nemeroff, Brenda Ferreira and my extended family: you are the sturdy patches in my life's vase.

To my beloved husband, Dan, and my children, Grant and Jody, for letting me tell our stories and for filling my life with love, joy and song.

And finally, a special thank you to co-spirit, Jimmy Laura Smull—the best fellow traveler one could wish for in life.

CAROL ORSBORN, PH.D.

On Becoming Wise

During the course of our research, we conversed with over one hundred women who are demonstrating a remarkable capacity to take whatever life brings their way as an opportunity for personal growth. Defying stereotypes of aging, both individually and as a group, women in their late forties, fifties, sixties and beyond are achieving psychological and spiritual mastery in multiple areas of their lives. There is the growing sense that as a generation, we are reinventing expectations about the quality of our futures, not only for ourselves but also for those to come. We are, in fact, becoming wise.

This spontaneous attunement is quite palpable. Our research identified the early signs of a grassroots movement that has the potential for personal and societal transformation. We are, after all, the generation that rose up against the mythology of the perfect woman of the 1950s. We gave birth to the women's liberation movement. As young adults, we took on an array of traditional institutions, including politics and religion. Most recently, we transformed hot flashes into power surges. Now, we are turning the page on our journey to wisdom and mastery. We are challenging our parents' notion of aging and waking up to the need and the potential for taking charge of our destinies.

OUTDATED NOTIONS

Our parents' generation thought that aging meant a world in which a depressing decline was inevitable. They were old at 50. They looked old. They acted old.

Historians teach us that our parents' concept of old age finds its roots in the years immediately following World War II. Women and older people had played a vital role in keeping the country running while the men were away. Then they were prevailed upon to step aside at war's end to make room for the returning heroes. Those who failed to cooperate were labeled cranky, eccentric or even senile. Stereotypes die hard. And so it is that today we still face a hostile landscape populated by news reports, advertisements and advisers eager to frighten us with breathless reports of hidden dangers and troubles ahead.

The news is not that these messengers of ill tidings continue to reinforce the stereotypes of aging. Rather, the scoop is that so many of the women of our generation question the premise that aging is a problem and the future something to fear. The fact is that no one really knows what's in store for any of us, now or further down the road. This is particularly pertinent for our generation, considering that in 1900, not long before many of our own mothers were born, the average American woman lived to be only 47.3 years of age. Today, many of us will have four decades or more of quality life ahead of us, not only living longer, but in better health and with more vitality. We take advantage of medical and technological breakthroughs. We instinctively pace ourselves for longer life spans that are now the norm rather than the exception. Given the size of our demographic, we are capable of making a big impact on our society today and in the coming decades—economically, politically and socially. Moreover, when viewed through the lens of developmental theory, the fact of our magnitude, coupled with the aggregate length of our lives, creates the potential for an unprecedented number of us to scale the heights of personal growth, achieving an advanced stage of life mastery, honed by many seasons of experience.

THE SILVER PEARL

Is it any wonder, given our history and potential, that we are transcending outdated expectations? That we are determining a meaningful and creative life for ourselves, at once both practical and visionary? The answer is found in the pages ahead. We use the metaphor of the silver pearl to describe the state of advanced psychological and spiritual attainment.

In the course of our research for this book, we conversed with women in our generation who have achieved this heightened stage of wisdom and life mastery in one or more areas of their lives. What is more remarkable is that they are doing so even while taking care of declining parents, preparing for the future or any of the ten top issues that emerged from our research. As a generation, we quite simply don't relate to what many theorists refer to as "the problems of aging." Rather, our research indicates that we continue to be interested in addressing the same concerns that have always captured our generation's attention: how to find meaning, be productive, establish healthy relationships, reduce stress, make a contribution to society and relish the fully-lived life.

As the two of us turned from research to writing, we found ourselves eager to communicate what we are learning with others who are also noticing that something extraordinary is happening with our generation of women. Even more importantly, we look forward to continuing our conversation with those of us who are actually living the experience.

We feel blessed to have the opportunity to share what we have learned with you as together, our journey to the silver pearl unfolds!

CAROL ORSBORN, PH.D.

JIMMY LAURA SMULL, PH.D.

AUGUST 2005, LOS ANGELES, CALIFORNIA

PART ONE

The Legend of the Silver Pearl

I n the spiritual traditions of the ancient east, there is the story of a young girl who wanted, above all, to discover the secret to the meaning of life. Her mother, aware of her daughter's yearning, sent her to the oldest, wisest woman in her village to ask for advice.

"What must I do to find the treasure I seek?" the girl asked the wise woman. The two sat in silence for many moments, and then the wise woman replied.

"Far, far away, on the other side of the sea, you will find a mountain cave nestled in the foothills. In the cave, there is a silver pearl. Retrieve the pearl, and you will have the answer you seek."

The girl packed her boat, and courageously set out to find the priceless pearl. She rowed for many hours across the sea until finally she spied the mountain cave. Climbing to the opening, she was at last able to peer inside. Squinting into the darkness, she saw a large, silver pearl glistening brightly through the shadows of the cave. But as her eyes adjusted, she saw, too, that the pearl was tightly clasped in the claws of a huge, ferocious dragon. For several days and nights, the young girl hid behind a rock at the entrance, plotting and planning schemes to retrieve the pearl. But the dragon held firm, and eventually the girl gave up and returned home, reconciling herself to living her everyday life.

Over the years, she grew into a lovely young woman, so busy meeting life's demands that she forgot about the silver pearl. First there was the completion of her studies and the arrangement of her marriage to a suitable young man. There was the deepening of their relationship into love as they spent long hours side-by-side, tilling the fields and milking the cows. Then there were her babies—first steps, childhood games and studies, courting and marriages of their own, children no more. Along the way, there were the inevitable losses, the deaths of her mother and father, and years of good crops and bad. And now, at last, she thought again of the silver pearl.

Without a moment's hesitation, she took up her oars and set out across the sea for the mountain cave. She rowed for many hours until, at last, she stood at the opening, peering once more into the darkness. The large, silver pearl radiated in the shadows. But as her *eyes adjusted, she saw something even more wondrous, indeed. While the dragon still clutched the pearl tightly, the once fearsome beast had shrunken to the size of a harmless lizard. She easily plucked the pearl from its grip and carried it home.*

The fierce battle that she'd plotted in her youth had been fought and won inside herself as she met the challenges of her daily life. It was not really the dragon that had diminished. It was she who had grown in inner strength and stature. She had found the treasure in the living of her life.

―――――――

Long ago, you, too, began your search for the silver pearl. Faced with fearsome dragons, frustrated by your shortcomings, you returned to your everyday life. Over time, your quest for the treasure receded before the pressures of more immediate concerns.

You were not alone.

Our generation of women has found our days challenging and busy, as we established thriving careers and loving relationships. We raised families and took care of our declining parents. We worked hard, keeping ourselves vitally energetic and engaged. Even the most accomplished of us have faced illness, financial setbacks, loneliness and loss.

At last, in the midst of our seasoned lives, we are growing wise. Honed by many years of experience, we look for time to fulfill a commitment made long ago, requiring more of us than we ever suspected we'd have to give. The once fearsome dragon that guarded the silver pearl has retreated to the shadows. At long last, we find ourselves empowered to reach out for something wondrous and unexpected: an unshakable inner core, forged out of everything that has happened to us, our triumphs as well as our tragedies.

The Legend of *The Silver Pearl* delivers a message that is simple but transformational: unlike physical development, the older you become, the more possible is it for you to achieve your fullest potential. In this, age is our ally. We find ourselves increasingly able to embrace life's incongruities. We are comfortable with a core identity, one that is trustworthy and balanced.

It is this state that we symbolize with the silver pearl: an experience of ourselves and the world at this unique juncture in history, in which we have the unprecedented opportunity to harvest the gifts of life and time. The communal wisdom of our generation is redefining not only our own, but society's notions of who we are and what is possible—for ourselves as well as the world. This is the power that comes from psychological and spiritual growth throughout the course of our lives.

As researchers studying women who are increasing their mastery of life as the years unfold, we are witnesses to this renewed excitement regarding life's possibilities. Regardless of the trials and challenges our participants have encountered, many are reaching milestone birthdays feeling more vital, smarter and stronger than they had ever anticipated.

SECRET KNOWLEDGE

Not only do we have more time to learn and grow, but our generation has had unprecedented access to an inventory of sources and information about life mastery drawn from many other times and places. What in other societies would have constituted "secret knowledge," ancient texts garbed in esoteric language and obtuse imagery available only to an elite, is readily available to us. We can try it out in our every day lives, often at the click of a mouse. We have a vivid sense of what an advanced psychological and spiritual experience of life can be, and we have extended time to weave our discoveries into our core identities. As a generation of seekers, we have a unique opportunity to commit to personal growth, to achieve the advanced stages of wisdom and life mastery represented by the silver pearl: wholeness, experienced at its peak as holiness.

THE FORMATION OF THE PEARL

Through the centuries, pearls have been sought for their physical beauty and symbolic value. For the ancient Romans, the pearl represented purity and love. The early Christians used pearls as a metaphor for the attainment and safeguarding of personal merit. In eastern traditions, the pearl served as the symbol of wisdom. It is not the pearl, itself, that has inspired humanity's highest aspirations.

Rather, it is how a pearl is formed.

You may recall Anne Morrow Lindbergh's description in her book, *Gift from the Sea*: The oyster shell is "untidy, spread out in all directions, heavily encrusted with accumulations... It suggests the struggle of life itself." The simple oyster, one would have to agree, is the least likely of creatures to produce such a magnificent creation as a pearl. But it does. The struggle to form a pearl begins when a foreign body enters the oyster's shell. If unable to expel the threat, the oyster secretes an iridescent substance, which gradually hardens into a protective cover around the intruder. The pearl grows out of the oyster's efforts to protect itself—a wondrous synthesis of resilience and beauty.

The formation of a pearl is a metaphor for ongoing psychological and spiritual development. It is reflected in the life stories of the women in our study. It is rooted in the fields of cultural mythology and rituals, enabling us to identify predictable sequences of personal growth through which women are likely to progress on their way to life mastery.

THE POTENTIAL TO PROGRESS

According to cultural mythology, we begin our progression through life with the full potential to love, to find meaning, to feel good about the world and ourselves. Inevitably, however, from the moment we leave mother's womb, we are greeted with frustrations, discomforts and all manner of discrepancy between what we want and what we are getting. Along with physical discomforts come messages, influences and experiences that run counter to our innate sense of who we are and how we expect things to be. Some of the messages are positive and helpful, but many are painfully imposed on us, alien to our own innate beliefs, behaviors and expectations.

As awareness of this discomfort reaches critical mass, we begin rejecting the agendas others have imposed on us. We must do so to define, face and master our challenges in a way that feels authentic. We enter a period of dynamic creativity. And, like the oyster's pearl, much of it is formed in reaction to influences we no longer wish to have operating in our lives.

Given sufficient time and intention, we have the opportunity to move beyond the victimization of the first stage and the reactivity and rebelliousness of the second to achieve the ultimate state of psychological and spiritual development that we associate with the silver pearl.

As precious as all pearls are, silver pearls carry added symbolic value. Synthesizing black and white into a gray that shines as silver, as if illuminated from within, these are pearls of a rare hue that contain both light and shadow. This luminescent silver is a symbol for a life that embraces greater complexity. It reflects what it means to be fully alive and authentic specifically because it does not leave anything out, neither triumph nor tragedy. The silver pearl is an apt representation of the highest stage of personal development. Ultimately, the essential task is not to ignore or forget our pasts, nor to judge ourselves harshly for the behaviors and beliefs we incorporated into our lives as the best responses we could muster at the time, but rather, to embrace our personal histories with compassion. Each of us who has claimed the silver pearl for herself expresses in her own special way the profound joy that comes from melding together all aspects of life into something at once authentically old and brand new.

By learning to embrace it all, we gain everything we need to retrieve the silver pearl. With great patience, it has been waiting for our return. Shall we continue?

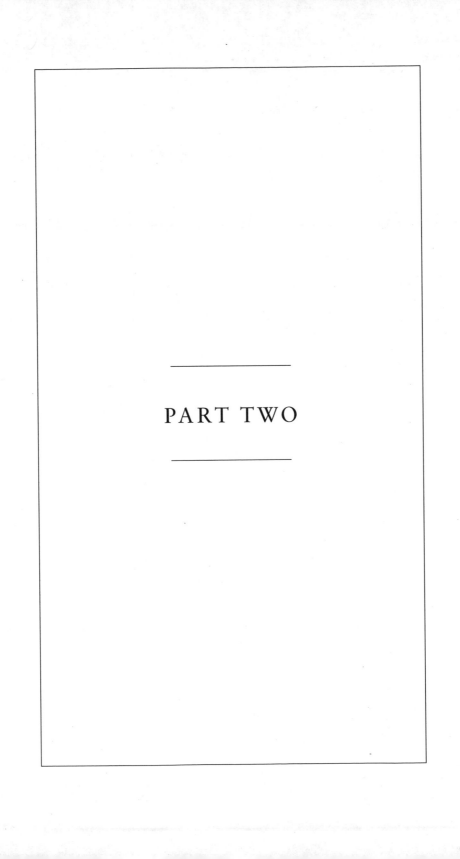

PART TWO

Your Silver Pearl Wisdom Inventory

When you were young, you knew that you were born to manifest your full potential to love, to find meaning, to feel good about yourself and the world. In order to claim your destiny, you were sure that you needed only to reach out and grab the prize that was already yours. But along the way, you inevitably encountered obstacles. At times, you found yourself feeling hopeless, believing that you were the only one in the world who knew what it meant to suffer.

Anna, an artist famous for her paintings of peaceful domestic scenes, took a step outside her gallery opening to whisper a heartfelt question to us.

"Do you ever wonder why it is that you can be so successful in some areas of your life, and yet have areas where you just can't seem to get it together?"

Anna and her manager, Stephanie, had just agreed to participate in one of our research circles, a series of discussions with over 100 women who had achieved mastery in one or more areas of their lives. Despite her concerns, we knew that Anna more than qualified as a role model.

For decades, Anna's bucolic watercolors were icons for our generation of women, showing how we always expected our lives to turn out. But on the day of the research circle, it became apparent that her life was anything but simple. Before much time passed, she shared with the other participants a long list of concerns: everything from issues with her weight and failed investments; to worries about a needy mother; loneliness; and a grown daughter, who, despite having recently gotten a decent job, refused to leave the nest.

While we were listening, her manager, Stephanie, suddenly cut in: "Anna! So what's new? As long as I've known you, you've been complaining about your mother, your finances, your children, your love life, your weight, just to name a few!"

Stephanie's observation rang true, not only for Anna, but for many of us in the room. None of us could deny that our lives, our circumstances, our relationships keep going through changes. The question is: *When haven't our lives been going through changes?*

While many of us might prefer to be settling down into some kind of serene status, we have come to the conclusion that the very fact of our discontent is a sign that something extraordinary is happening with our generation of women. What do we mean by this?

Until our generation of women hit midlife and beyond, the prevailing assumption in psychological circles was that at our age, we should already have pretty much arrived at our developmental destinations. We should be humble harvesters of the seeds we've sown in the past—for better or for worse—but no longer creators of our destinies. We did say "until recently." That is because as some of our classic scholars began to age, they started championing the notion of lifelong development.

What they found, and what our research supported, is that just as there are normal stages of physical development for human beings, so are there normal stages of psychological, emotional, social and spiritual development. As we grow through life experiences, we advance through a predictable sequence of stages. If you miss going through a stage along the way, you've got to go back and fill it in or—consciously or unconsciously—you will be stuck at the stage in the particular area where your development stalled. The revolutionary aspect of this lifelong development concept is that progression through the stages does not necessarily need to occur at any particular age. And moreover, unlike physical development, the older you become, the more possible it is for you to achieve your fullest potential. (For more about this, see *Theoretical Grounding* in the Appendix.)

The fact that Anna and so many others in our research circle expressed discontent in one or more areas of their lives is far from an indication of a personal shortcoming. Discontent is but one of many signs that we are still growing, still striving and most important of all, still dreaming about the fulfillment of life's promise. Refusing to go quietly into submissive old age, we are becoming free in ways that we did not anticipate, taking an active role in determining our own experience of life and, along the way, reinventing the future for ourselves.

To reclaim your own destiny, there is but one caveat: You must become a truth teller, willing to scrutinize your most familiar notions about how the world works. You can do this by taking on the challenging but rewarding task of stripping away your false understandings. Then you can uncover and integrate the bits and pieces of meaning, waiting patiently for you beneath the surface of your life, into a whole. Like the archeologist ready to go to work with her shovel and pick, the critical task is to figure out where to dig. As many of the women in our study have discovered, the answer is simple but unappealing: you must be willing to turn *towards* rather than *away from* the uncomfortable and unresolved issues in your life.

When you do, you will discover that there is nothing that life has brought you that you can't handle. As certain aspects of your life are receding, others are advancing, breathing new life into your all-but-forgotten dreams. So it is that we make progress in our lives, leaving behind old beliefs, behaviors and situations that no longer serve us, and acquiring new depths of awareness about who we are becoming.

In a moment, you will be taking The Silver Pearl Wisdom Inventory that will show you your achievements, your progress and your remaining vulnerabilities on an issue-by-issue basis. Before you do, there are some important points to keep in mind.

For one thing, very few of the women who have taken this assessment have achieved the highest level of development across the board. In fact, it is not only possible but likely that you will discover yourself be at one stage of development in one area of your life, and at a completely different stage in another. This is due, in part, to the fact that because of the way you were brought up, you are likely to have gotten stuck in or skipped various stages of development, finding yourself stalled in one or more areas.

While we may wish to seek a short cut, developmental psychology teaches us that in order to advance, you've got to go back and complete the tasks of the missing stages before moving on. This is good news, however. For whatever your age may be, it is never too late to fill in the missing gaps. The goal is to progress through all life stages in as many issue areas as possible, preparing yourself for, rather than reacting to, the situations that life brings your way. After you've taken the following self-assessment, you will be provided with an interpretation of your responses, a helpful guide to the 100 readings in Part Three.

Keep track of the answer that best completes the sentence for each issue that applies to your personal situation. You may record more than one answer. At the end of the assessment, we will tell you how to interpret your responses.

With regard to...
Preparing for the future, I:
Stage 1 Worry about what lies ahead.

Stage 2 Am obsessed with what I need to do, or deny the need to do anything about even obvious, practical matters.

Stage 3 Combine faith and planning to address realistic possibilities.

Ambition, I:
Stage 1 Fall short of expectations.

Stage 2 Redouble my efforts to achieve my goals, either exhausting myself or giving up.

Stage 3 Achieve self-acceptance of both my strengths and limitations, continuing to set and work towards goals, without allowing them to drive me to injure myself.

Love and relationships, I:
Stage 1 View toxic relationships with past, current or potential mates/friends/relatives as the norm.

Stage 2 Try too hard and settle for less than I deserve, or generally turn my back on the possibility of love.

Stage 3 Make choices that are loving and forgiving, but self-protective.

Parenting grown children, I:
Stage 1 Perceive my children's success to be a reflection of my own self-worth.

Stage 2 Hang on to unhealthy ways of relating, or disown my relationship with them entirely.

Stage 3 Accept a new, healthier relationship with my grown children and relish my own independence.

With regard to...
Unfinished business,
including both regrets and unfulfilled goals, **I:**

Stage 1 Am unable or unwilling to address past issues.

Stage 2 Feel open-ended guilt, shame or regret.

Stage 3 Pursue my dreams and find closure by making appropriate amends.

Beauty, I:

Stage 1 Define success in life by my looks.

Stage 2 Strive for perfection or let myself go.

Stage 3 Enjoy being my best possible self, within the context of my age and circumstances.

Health, I:

Stage 1 Think of illness as a shortcoming or as punishment.

Stage 2 Fret excessively, or become neglectful of my body's needs.

Stage 3 Do what I can to stay healthy, knowing that while some things are out of my control, the best possible outcome is always something for which I can work and hope.

Inevitabilities,
including caregiving, loss and mortality, **I:**

Stage 1 Relate to decline and death as something to be feared, or as a sign of personal failure.

Stage 2 Become hyper-vigilant, or deny others' as well as my own mortality.

Stage 3 Deal responsibly with the issues as they arise, taking time to mourn the losses and establishing a healthy regard for my own mortality.

Creating a legacy, I:

Stage 1 Believe life is measured by external standards.

Stage 2 Deny the impact I make every day.

Stage 3 Recognize my potential to influence the world without concern about getting credit.

With regard to...
Meaning, I:

Stage 1 Remain dissatisfied, wondering what's wrong with me that I just can't be happy with what I have.

Stage 2 Rage against my sense of meaningless or ignore my deep, diffuse yearnings.

Stage 3 Cultivate acceptance of life's mysteries, embracing others and myself with compassion.

STAGE 1: ORIGINAL PROGRAMMING

If you gave yourself a Stage 1 response in any (or multiple) category, you have taken the courageous first step of admitting to yourself that in some areas of your life, you have lost important parts of your original, authentic self. It has been buried beneath the beliefs, judgments and limitations imposed upon you by others.

This sense of loss is predicated on the understanding that human beings are born with the capacity to experience awe and wonder, to love fully and deeply and to express themselves without filters. However, you are inevitably burdened with messages, influences and experiences that run counter to your innate sense of yourself, programming you to have limited expectations about how things can be.

To the degree that you were trained to deny your real thoughts, feelings and needs, you find yourself living in a world of superficial meanings, in which you are urged to act, perform, and consume as expected.

If you gave a Stage 1 response in any of the ten areas in the self-assessment, there is hidden programming from your past that is likely to have been embedded in your response. Know that the moment you make a conscious effort to recognize the hidden message, you begin making up lost ground.

STAGE 2: THE REACTIVE RESPONSE

If you gave a Stage 2 response to any (or multiple) issue in the self-assessment, you have already come to realize that the messages you received earlier in your life are not always in sync with your own beliefs and values. During this stage, you are literally "dis-illusioned," not only about the people and messages that have previously determined your reality—but about the way you have always pictured yourself to be: the good daughter, the faithful wife, the community leader, and so on.

You know you are in Stage 2 if your new beliefs and behaviors come about primarily as a response to influences you no longer want or need in your life. This explains why Stage 2 responses can often seem to oppose each other, gravitating to the poles of denial at one end of the spectrum, or rebellion at the other. However your response mechanisms play out, it is the recognition of your own reactivity—not the style, intensity or content—that determines that you are, indeed, still in Stage 2 and have not yet arrived at your final destination.

As the old conceptions pass away, signs of new beliefs and behaviors formed in reaction to them begin to emerge. You will know that you are back on track to making real progress when you become aware not only of what others have done to you, but what your own self-protective reactions have done to yourself.

As you make the transition from Stage 2 to Stage 3, you will begin to feel more prepared than ever to handle whatever challenges come your way. You will find yourself able to address and resolve issues that have been weighing you down all your life.

STAGE 3: THE SILVER PEARL

If you gave yourself a Stage 3 on any (or multiple) issue, you have achieved the most advanced stage of development—the stage we call The Silver Pearl. In the first two stages of psychological and spiritual growth—Original Programming and Reactive Responses—it is natural to react emotionally to limiting and self-damaging beliefs.

When you have achieved The Silver Pearl, this third and highest phase of development, the essential task is not to ignore or forget your past, nor to judge yourself harshly for behaviors and beliefs you incorporated into your life as the best response you could muster at the time, but rather, to make peace with your personal history. This does not mean that you surrender any of your personal power out of misplaced loyalty, guilt or fear. But rather, that you use everything you've got—including your past—to fuel your personal growth.

This is the essence of resolution: the thoughtful, gentle melding together of something authentic and unshakable. In Stage 3, we have the opportunity to complete the unfinished work of both the Original Programming and Reactive Responses Stages, regardless of whatever age we happen to be. The task is to establish a mature relationship with the worldviews of our earliest authority figures, then attend to the fulfillment of life's promise.

PART THREE

One Hundred Readings

Far, far away, on the other side of the sea, you will find
a mountain cave nestled in the foothills. In the cave, there is
a silver pearl. Retrieve the pearl, and you will have
the answer you seek.

You are invited to engage with the following readings, which are grouped into the ten issues most frequently cited by the women in our research. The readings synthesize psychological research, spiritual principles and common sense drawn from a range of eastern and western influences. Most importantly, many of them communicate the wisdom and stories of our research participants—women who have achieved The Silver Pearl stage in one or more areas of their lives. As members of this generation of women, we have contributed elements of our own personal stories and inspiration, as well.

Within each of the ten sections, the readings are strategically arranged to guide you through the three stages of psychological and spiritual growth we introduced earlier. We suggest that you begin by turning first to the issue that is foremost on your mind, paying particular attention to any of those issues in Your Silver Pearl Wisdom Inventory to which you gave yourself a Stage 1 or 2 response. By engaging with the readings that pertain to that particular issue, you will be led through a dynamic process of personal growth.

As the readings in each of the sections progress, you will be able to identify where you are relying on outdated coping tools to deal with issues of the present and future. As you read on, you will gain access to new tools and perspectives, leading you towards the stage of wisdom and life mastery we symbolize with the silver pearl.

The most instructive finding from our research is that advancement to the highest levels of psychological and spiritual attainment does not occur simultaneously across the board. Rather it comes on an issue-by-issue basis. In fact, it is not only possible, but likely, that you will discover yourself to be at one stage of development in one area of your life, and at a completely different stage in another.

We are works-in-progress, with time enough to make advances in every area of our lives. This is welcome news, indeed, as after conversations with 100 participants, we concluded that given everything that's happening in our lives, personal power and spiritual proficiency can no longer be considered a luxury.

For those who are interested, the Appendix to this book provides additional background on the theory behind the stages of psychological and spiritual development that provide the framework for the progression of readings in Part Two.

You have it within your power to attain The Silver Pearl, to increase life mastery and meaning. We ask only one thing of you: that you engage the readings with an open mind, as well as an open heart.

Preparing
for the Future

When you find yourself thinking about the future, your first impulse is
    to feel anxious.
    "Should I be doing more? Is my survival at stake? Why do I feel
    so unprepared?"

Thinking of yourself as a realist, you brace yourself for the worst,
    your efforts fueled by the fierce determination to rise to the occasion.

All the while, your soul cries out to you,
    asking you to trade the illusion of control for the richness
    of the fully lived life.

Of course you should do what you can to address your concerns,
    but remember to leave room for the possibility
    that good things happen, too,
    often when you are least expecting it.

1
Come As You Are

Y ou've worked hard to get where you are. You're smart.
You're strategic. And yet suddenly you find yourself feeling
vulnerable about the future, less than prepared for the
challenges ahead.

A week before our first research circle, one of our participants
called to tell us that her mother had just received word that she was
to undergo life-threatening surgery. Celia called in her regrets,
asking us to keep her upsetting news confidential. We were
disappointed and concerned for Celia and her mother, but of course,
we understood.

On the morning of our gathering Celia called, asking if she
could come after all.

"Had the surgery gone well?"

"It's not scheduled until next week. We still don't know."

We assured Celia that we could reschedule her for a future time,
but she was insistent.

"The thing is, I realized that the main reason I felt I couldn't
come was that I knew you were talking to people who could serve
as role models. I wanted you to think of me as the together
businesswoman who lets nothing faze her. And yet here I was,
canceling a session I'd been looking forward to, asking you to keep
secrets and throwing myself into work so as to not have to deal
with my feelings."

Celia paused, taking a deep breath. "Then I suddenly realized
that I was, indeed, letting something faze me. Ironically, it was none
other than my concern that I would appear to be untogether. So
bottom line: if you still think I'm a role model, and let me come as I
am, I'll be there."

Celia came and her contribution was enormous. What she
taught us was that the first step in facing the future is admitting to
yourself the whole truth about what you're really feeling, without

thinking that you necessarily need to do anything about it. The emotions you are experiencing are not your obstacles. In fact, the secret to making the best possible decisions is to let your heart break open. Clarity, insight and hope enter through these cracks of vulnerability. Embrace the broader range of the human experience: bittersweet sadness, genuine concern and yes, even anxiety about the road that lies ahead. Come as you are, and insight will come to you as a by-product of your honest response to life's summons.

2
You're Not Alone

———◦●◦———

Y ou think you're the only one who feels unprepared for the future. So, you present a brave front to outsiders lest they judge you to be inadequate.

Unbeknownst to you—while you were figuring out how to pay for your children's college educations, worrying about the rise and fall of the stock market, and rushing to stay abreast of the increasing needs of your aging parents—our entire generation of women was doing the same things.

Here's a plan. Call eight friends and invite them over to talk— not about little complaints that are suitable for networking lunches, but a real, honest to God, let your hair down session where everybody's saga is welcome and nobody is judged. *Your savings aren't where you think they should be, and the thought is dawning on you that you will need to work forever? The younger people at work are eyeing your job like a hungry pack of wolves? Your mother won't use her hearing aid and you've got a sore throat from shouting?* Whine, cry, laugh. Don't set out to solve anything. You don't need answers. What you—what we all need—right now is to know that we're in this together and that together, we will somehow make it through.

3
Patch a Labyrinth

———●———

Her youngest child, Jody, was just heading off to college, and after nearly twenty years of being held hostage by school districts, Carol and her husband were finally able to move to the little cottage of their dreams in one of the hilly canyons above Los Angeles. On one of her early explorations in the steep hills behind their cottage, she'd stumbled across a labyrinth built out of rocks by hands unknown. It seemed positively miraculous.

Labyrinths have a rich, spiritual history. In places like Chartres Cathedral in France, contemplatives since medieval times have silently walked the sacred geometry of the labyrinth's serpentine route. The reward was usually renewed peace of mind.

Never would Carol need that sacred path of rocks more than that first year. Not only did her last child leave home, but suddenly her father passed away, thrusting her into her new, challenging role as caretaker to a grieving, increasingly incapacitated mother. The labyrinth became Carol's place of refuge—walking a truth deeply into her bones: that there are things in our lives that are simply not in our power to control.

Then the winter rains came. Unable to negotiate the river of mud that poured off the hills, Carol was unable to renew her spirit by visiting her beloved labyrinth. By the time the sun reappeared, she was anxious about nearly everything. *Was there another boot just waiting to drop? Do I really have what it takes to make it through this difficult time? Will my sadness never end?* By the time she was finally able to climb the hill, she had added a new worry to her already long list of concerns: *Would my labyrinth still be there?*

In dread, she mounted the final few steps.

What she saw next took her breath away. Not only had the labyrinth survived the deluge—it had been fully restored. Unknown hands had lovingly replaced each and every rock.

Carol immediately understood the error in her thinking. Given the year's profound losses, she had accepted her powerlessness, embracing the fact that you can't always stop bad things from happening. But now, witnessing the restored labyrinth, she realized something more. No matter how real our fears and concerns appear to us, surrendering the illusion of control means that you can't stop good things from happening, either.

4

Let Go of the Branch

——◼●◼——

A woman was taking a walk on a high mountain path when she slipped and saved herself from a precipitous fall by grabbing onto an overhanging branch. As the twelve-step story tells it, the woman was left dangling one hundred feet above the valley floor, when she suddenly felt the branch begin to crack.

This woman had never believed in God, but felt that this was as good a time as any to begin.

"God, are you up there?"

"Yes, my daughter," God replied. "What can I do for you?"

"God, help me. Tell me what to do!" she cried.

"You really want to know?"

The branch cracked a bit more.

Desperate, she cried out again.

"Yes, God. Tell me!"

There was a moment's silence. Then God answered her.

"Let go of the branch."

"Let go of the branch?"

"Yes, my daughter. Let go of the branch."

There was another moment's silence, then the woman spoke.

"Is there anybody else up there?"

5
Breathe

I t is not an accident that the ancient Hebrews used the same word for spirit as they did for breath: *Ruach*. Give your spirit a quick check-up right now by asking yourself: *Is my breathing rapid and shallow, or full and deep?* If you are feeling anxious, chances are that you are quite simply not getting enough air into your lungs. It is ironic that just when you need unobstructed access to your spirit most, your breathing is likely to become tight and quick, leaving you winded and depleted.

Here's an easy practice that will help you dig out from under anxiety. Start by thinking of a negative belief, opinion or concern about the future that you no longer want or need in your life. Breathe it slowly out.

Now, think of a quality you want more of in your life and breathe it in—slowly and deeply. As you continue breathing in, inhale life and light and the promise of the kind of future you truly deserve. As you continue to breathe out, let go of the anxiety and pain. Keep breathing slowly and deeply, knowing that the same life force that keeps the process of renewal alive in your body is fueling your spirit, as well.

6

Become Fully Vested in Yourself

When you were just out of college, and your parents told you to put your graduation money into a savings fund that would compound geometrically over the years— but you went to Europe, instead—some may have called you foolish. But others would see you as an adventurous spirit with an insatiable passion for living.

When you had children and you used every spare penny for their dance lessons and summer camps, some may have thought that money should have been invested in municipal stocks and bonds, but others would understand that you loved your children and wanted nothing more in life than for them to cultivate their talents and interests.

When all of your life, advertisements from blue chip financial companies told you to put enough away for a rainy day, you were the kind of person who instead put on a big pair of boots, and went outside to splash around.

Now you realize that your choices have had ramifications. Yes, you could have spent less and saved more. But before you buy into the notion of your recklessness, consider your decisions.

We're talking here about the investment you made in yourself and your family. For now, not despite of, but *because* of the decisions you made about time and money along the way, you are the kind of person who has an insatiable passion for living, a person who knows how to put her boots on and splash around in storms, a person whose children know how to dance.

7

Simply Do What's Next

———◖●◗———

There comes a time when you've opened your heart to others, you've laughed and you've cried, you've talked and you've listened. Inevitably, you've come to realize that while you may not be the best prepared in all the world for the future, you're not the least prepared, either. In fact, you know that you are making progress when you discover that talking about your worries regarding the future is beginning to be boring, even to yourself.

So now here's the key question: *What are you going to do about it?*

You've faced this question before. In fact, you wouldn't have made it this far if you weren't the kind of person who instinctively knows how to solve problems. Whether it pertained to locating a medical specialist or finding a new job after a merger, you knew that the first step always is to gather sufficient information upon which to make an informed decision. You put forth the effort to collect the opinions of all concerned. You assessed your options—and your deficiencies—and then you made and executed your plan.

You are, in fact, a champion decision-maker. So why is it that when it comes to "the future," your mind so frequently turns to mush?

For one thing, the word "future" sounds so real, it's easy to forget that the future doesn't exist yet. You will be more effective when you ask yourself exactly what it is about the future that is really bothering you. Answer each of the questions in order, spending at least several minutes per question, writing down every thought that comes into your mind.

If you're really stuck, not knowing which issue to pick first, here's some advice for you: start anywhere. The very process of beginning sets forces in motion that will bring you new clarity, courage, and perspective.

TEN QUESTIONS

1. What is the issue that worries me most about the future?
2. What outcome would I most like to achieve?
3. How have I tried to address this issue so far?
4. What was it about this approach that didn't work?
5. What information and/or emotional, spiritual, mental and physical resources do I need in order to bring about the resolution I seek?
6. What can I change?
7. What must I accept?
8. What is my greatest fear about this situation?
9. What is the truth about this situation?
10. What one thing am I willing to do now to address my concerns?

Answering these ten questions puts you back in the equation. You don't need to have everything figured out to make progress. All you need to know is what's next—and then, go do it.

8
Finding Lost Time

—•—

Consumed with the day-to-day affairs of her congregants, Laurie had never put much thought into her own future. She was rapidly approaching retirement age and becoming aware that the stipend her little rural church had scraped together for her was not going to cut it. Moreover, at sixty, while she was less and less willing to drive the hundreds of miles of dusty back roads to tend to her scattered flock, she still had things she wanted to do with her life. Laurie realized that after a lifetime of taking care of others, she would now have to go double or even triple time on her own behalf if she were ever to retire.

Like Laurie, many of us wake up to our inadequate preparation for the future with a sudden start, chased by our concerns into a state of panic. In the midst of her anxiety, Laurie's lifeline was Mary, an old seminary friend who had long ago taken a position with a wealthy suburban congregation overflowing with CPAs, lawyers and financial advisers. Laurie took the first flight out, anxious to meet with the advisers she trusted that Mary would have lined up, waiting to help her button down her affairs.

Instead, Mary greeted Laurie with a big hug and the key to the church's retreat cottage overlooking a secluded lake on the outskirts of the acreage. Mary's only advice to Laurie: that she spend as long as she needed in a state of quiet contemplation until she felt confident again. Reluctantly, Laurie took the key, certain she was only wasting even more valuable time.

For the first several days in retreat, she wrote down pages and pages of concerns. After a few more days, she heard a bird singing for the first time and noticed that there were little waves gently lapping against the shore just feet from her front door. At the end of her first week, she began remembering how little she really needed in her life to make her happy: some good books, simple meals and long nature walks. Around that time, she noticed that her panic had subsided and that she was thinking more clearly.

At the end of her second week of retreat, she sought out Mary, excited about the plan that had snuck up on her while she had been half asleep...an old dream that had been nearly forgotten in her mad rush to take matters into her own hands.

"I'd always had it in the back of my mind that someday I would love to be the spiritual director of a retreat center. I'd have a place to live. But more importantly, I could continue to work—and in a position where my capacity to perform will actually be enriched rather than compromised by my age. What do you think?"

That very afternoon, Mary connected Laurie with the director of a retreat center who was looking for somebody to start as soon as possible. The last time we spoke, Laurie was packing her bags and heading off to her new post.

Of course, there are things you could and should be doing that will help ensure that you make the most of the years ahead. But thinking about her initial panicky reaction, Laurie realized that the problem with making up for lost time is that it is so easy to lose touch with the present. You want to do everything within your power to envision your future as peaceful and comfortable—but meanwhile, in your efforts to achieve this worthwhile goal, you let yourself become frenzied and pressured today.

When you are afraid, it's easy to forget that it's not only *what* you put in place for your future—it's *how* you go about doing it.

If you want peace in your future, why not be peaceful today? If you want more love in your future, why not be more loving today? If you want more faith in your future, why not have more faith now?

9

Turn Your Complaints into Prayers

Perhaps it is time to consider the possibility that your grievances could go to a place where they could do some good.

Where is this place? Send them to the heart of the universe, where unlimited possibilities can engage your concerns in ways that are beyond your comprehension.

Here's how. Make note of any of the complaints and issues that are looping through your mind. *I'm not where I should be at this point. What if I do my best and still come up short? Clearly, I need help!* Now write them down, simply inserting your name for the divine periodically, and an "Amen" at the end. For practice, go ahead and fill in the blank.

Dear _____, I'm not where I should be at this point.
What if I do my best and still come up short?
Clearly, I need help. Amen.

By addressing your grievances to a power greater than yourself, you transform your worries into supplications, inviting divine compassion to soften the edges of your concerns, turning infinite grievance into infinite possibilities.

In the words of Larry Dossey, a doctor who applied scientific research to the efficacy of prayer on his patients: "In its simplest form, prayer is an attitude of the heart—a matter of being, not doing. Prayer is the desire to contact the Absolute, however it may be conceived. When we experience the need to enact this connection, we are praying, whether or not we use words."

Oddly enough, you don't have to believe that this works for it to be effective. You don't even have to feel worthy for it to work. In fact, there is a rich mystical tradition that contends that it is your very awareness of your undeservedness that makes your prayer potent. In the texts of many faith traditions, it is often the unlikeliest candidate who is afforded the benefits of prayer. A sheepherder, stuttering on a mountaintop. A beggar woman, reaching out secretly to touch a sacred hem.

There appears to be something infinitely compelling about authentically struggling with your concerns, while simultaneously finding the capacity to reach out from the depths of your soul for help.

10
Work-in-Progress: A Checklist

- When you need help, do you know how to get it?
- When you are faced with uncertainties, do you have the inner resources to persevere?
- When you want to do everything you can, do you understand that "everything" includes taking the time for introspection?

If so, then your future is already a work in progress, being painted by the brush of your spirit every time you choose faith over fear.

PREPARING FOR THE FUTURE

THE FEAR
*The future is a dangerous place
and my worries are justified.*

THE TRUTH
*Surrendering control over the unknown
means that I can't stop good things from happening, either.*

Ambition

As much as you have accomplished,
   you sense that there is something more yet for you to do.
Even your string of successes may chide you with having fallen short
   of what is expected of you—of fulfilling your potential.

Often, you respond by prodding yourself to once more rise
   to the occasion,
      even if the pressured pursuit of your goals injures you
      or others along the way.
Sometimes, you deny the urges that beckon you to make an effort,
   giving up with salty tears.

There is another way.
For on the path that truly counts—the path to increased wisdom,
   love and knowledge—the task before you is
   to use your ambition as a forum for the evolution of your spirit.

Every day provides many opportunities for such greatness.
In truth, the experience of success you've been seeking cannot be
   seized by force,
      but unfolds spontaneously as a by-product of who you become
      along the way, while you are living your life.

11

To What Do You Give Your Heart?

———◗●◖———

Many of us admire the lyrical, larger than life flowers of the artist Georgia O'Keefe. But did you know that shortly after the turn of the century, the talented young painter dropped out of formal art training? Georgia could no longer force herself to paint in the style of the times. It was a formalistic genre that felt alien to her. Regretfully, she laid down her brushes, certain that her own artistic sensibilities would never win the respect of the art community.

Four years later, thinking her years as an artist were behind her, she enrolled in a summer course for art teachers. There, seated side-by-side with fellow students, she listened with rapt attention as the instructor introduced her to a revolutionary notion: that the goal of art is to give expression to the artist's personal ideas and feelings. Reanimated, Georgia began experimenting with deeply individual styles, mediums and subject matters—a lifelong journey that she continued well into her 90s. Even when critics assailed her and her deeply feminine flowers and landscapes, she remained true to her vision. When failing eyesight eventually forced her to abandon painting, she took up pencil and watercolor. And then, even with her health continuing to decline, she used the tactile senses that remained in her fingers to sculpt in clay.

Georgia's vision was great, and her accomplishments breathtaking. But the scope and magnitude are not what moves us most. Rather, it is Georgia's courage and freedom—her refusal to settle for a pale imitation of herself imposed upon her by others, and her on-going commitment to stay true to her authentic voice, regardless of the consequences.

Enroute to trying to be "good"—setting out to win the admiration and respect of others—many of us have allowed our innate ambition to become overlaid by other people's expectations.

One who felt this way was Melina, a professional speaker at her professional peak. She arrived at a luncheon interview with us exhausted by the demands of her success. "Everybody thinks what I'm doing is so cool. But they weren't standing next to me at my bedside this morning hearing me say: 'God you must have a different plan for me. I've given this everything I've got and I hate my life.'"

Several months after our lunch with Melina, we followed up with her. She had news for us. "Right after we met, I signed up to go with a group on a spiritual retreat. The guide looked straight into my eyes and asked me: *If you could do anything in the world, what would it be?* Truth be told, I was furious with her, because taking her question seriously posed a threat to the investment I'd already made in my life, even if much of what I'd accomplished was at my own expense."

Recognizing fertile ground in her anger, Melina had to admit that the guide was onto something.

"Nevertheless, I couldn't deal with the question as she asked it. It was way too dangerous to me. But a few weeks after the retreat, I worked up the courage to try for something less grand, like: *If I could eat anything in the world, what would it be?* I had to struggle with even this, sorting through all the diets, nutritional advice and advertisements until I could uncover what I, Melina, most wanted to eat in the world. It turned out only to be chocolate covered raisins—but it was a beginning."

So to what do you want to give your heart and soul? The time has come for you to do something fresh, new, unexpected, daring—something that tests or challenges those who have laid claim upon you. Don't do it for sensation's sake—for the purpose of upsetting those around you. Rather, do it to reconnect to the voice in you that must not be denied.

12
Live Your Destiny

———●———

Once upon a time, a group of Lao-tzu's disciples were taking a walk in the woods. After several hours, they came across a clearing of many acres, where thousands of trees had been felled. In the very center was one particularly old, gnarly tree with many branches on it. Beneath it, the woodcutters rested in its shade.

"Why was this tree left standing?" The disciples inquired.

"Because it is absolutely useless," the woodcutters replied. "The bark is so tough, it breaks our saws. And even if we are able to chop off a piece, the smoke it makes when burned stings our eyes."

When the disciples reported this to Lao-tzu, he was delighted.

"Be like this tree. Be absolutely useless. If you become useful, somebody will come along and make a chair out of you. Be like this tree and you will be left alone to grow big and full, and thousands of people will come to rest under your shade."

It is tempting, indeed, to turn your life into a commodity. If you try simply to be useful, running around looking for your life. If you struggle to leave the largest inheritance, or secure the most enviable retirement, there will never be enough. If you try to live up to others' expectations, doing only what you should or ought, you will live anxiously, always worried about your future—and end up as a chair.

Take direction from your own heart, nurturing yourself along the way. Go for a walk in the middle of the day. Slowly enjoy a cup of tea. Remember sometimes to leave long spaces between thoughts. You will grow big and gnarly, your unique contribution coming about not in the pursuit of something great, but as you live your life day-by-day.

13
The Resilience Spiral

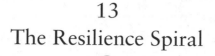

Popular motivational theory has taught us to think of success as a vertical climb from obscurity to prominence. In order to advance, we only need to call upon our will power to succeed in the relentless, single-minded drive to our goals. If we have to push through our fears and feelings, we do so. If we have to set aside our values or ignore the urge to take care of others or ourselves, so be it.

This linear model is powerful but problematical, and ultimately, doomed to fail. Why? Because the model only works when things are going your way. And the truth is, sooner or later, something is bound to go wrong in the pursuit of your goals, and will power alone cannot resolve it.

Happily, there is an alternative. Five thousand years ago, the ancient Chinese observed that reality is not linear but cyclical. We call our model based on cycles the Resilience Spiral. The Resilience Spiral captures the truth that everything in nature is in a constant state of change. Just when a season or stage reaches its peak, it inevitably turns into its opposite. The moon waxes and wanes. The mists rise and the rains fall.

So it is with your life. Right now, you may feel that autumn has bared your branches. Perhaps you find yourself in a place where your old ways of doing things no longer seem to work. But beneath the bark, even in the dead of winter, the sap is readying itself for rebirth in the spring. Sometimes, you are on the upswing, feeling the warmth of the sunlight opening your leaves. Other times, you are turned away, navigating the downward slope of the spiral. On these days you experience decay and dissolution. But in nature, destruction is often a requisite for new growth, like the pinecone bursting open in the heat of a forest fire, releasing its seeds to the soil.

And notice, too, this is not a circle—the endless repetition of beginnings and endings, going nowhere, accomplishing nothing. Rather, the Resilience Spiral expands, each upward turn of the spiral growing stronger, larger, fed by the enriched soil of your experiences, your learnings, and yes, even your setbacks. Rather than saying you will succeed, allowing nothing to get in your way, it is more accurate to say that you will do whatever it takes, understanding that many things are going to get in your way. On the Resilience Spiral everything can be used for growth—even descent.

14
Spring Forth

When a spring first gushes forth, it does not know where it is going. And yet, it bounds forward, rushing past, over and around boulders and logs until it meets the first deep place along its path. There, it tarries for as long as it takes, filling up the place that appears to be blocking its progress.

But nothing can trap the water for very long or alter its nature. When the time is right, the level will rise and the spring will overflow its banks, proceeding on its way.

The lesson is that you are where you are and it's alright. Your goals represent a commitment to a process, including success and failure. There will be times of rapid movement and times when you feel trapped.

Knowing that you want more for yourself does not invalidate what you already have. When you fall short, you can trust yourself to correct what you can and forgive yourself for what you can't. Your worthiness does not depend on your achievements or the things that happen to you. Your worthiness is not up for question.

The empty riverbed beyond beckons to you. If you just keep doing what's next, the time will come when you know where to go and how to get there. You will not have to drive yourself. Rather, you will tumble over the edge joyfully and discover that you are already on your way.

15
The Gift of Time

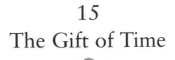

Claire lost her secure corporate job. With a few months of savings in the bank, she decided to take the opportunity to pursue her dream—setting up an interior design practice. For three years, she put concerted time and effort into establishing her business, and it took off. But year four was different. In the cold days of January, Claire was suddenly burdened by a nameless dread. Day after day, she pushed through the paces of running her business.

Desperate, she sought out an executive coach who gave her some startling advice. "The next time you approach your office, ask yourself how you are feeling. If you feel fine, proceed. If you are freaking out, don't go in. Just wait there and observe your feelings without judgment, for as long as it takes." Claire decided to try it out—and, indeed, it wasn't long before she found herself standing at the door to her office, letting the negative forces stop her.

Instead of berating herself for her lack of enthusiasm, she allowed herself simply to be curious: *"What is all this resistance about?"* Before too long, her thoughts were going to the stack of paperwork that awaited her, invoices to be sent out—and bills to be paid. Why wasn't she thinking about what she most enjoyed doing, sitting face-to-face with a client over samples and plans? Suddenly, she realized that the more successful she became, the more time she was spending making copies, sitting alone at her computer, scheduling appointments and deliveries. Of course—she wasn't dreading her work as an interior designer! She was dreading her work as an administrative assistant. It became obvious that what she needed was to hire someone to help her out. She threw open the office door and literally ran to her phone to place a help wanted ad.

If you pause while pushing through resistance, you will find that doing nothing is not always a waste of time. By emptying yourself of fear-driven effort, you make the space to receive information, insight and creative solutions that often are not available through action-oriented behavior. Trusting that larger forces than yourself are at work in your life, you will learn to make room for surprises. Learning to receive requires courage. Fueling your ambition through inspiration rather than by fear is the key.

16
The Fool

By the time we've reached midlife, we have tried many things. Many of us have unfulfilled dreams—the novel you tried to get published but sits languishing in your drawer; the promotion that you knew was yours, but went to the new recruit with a fancier degree. Of course, we learn from our failures and shortfalls. Voices of experience urge us to be more careful next time. These voices sometimes whisper—sometimes shout—but are always with us. They say take the lessons of the past and turn them into something sensible, realistic, responsible.

If you do, and if you are on fire with the joy of creation…if you can't wait to jump out of bed in the morning to continue on your journey…if you worry less about the future and more about how to capture the passion in your heart that you are feeling today…then the voices in your mind are your own, indeed: the mature expression of your wisdom made manifest.

But if this is not the case, beware! For if the knowledge you have gained from your life experiences is limiting your horizons rather than expanding them, you have confused resignation with acceptance, burnout with surrender. You are, in fact, using the notion of maturity and wisdom as an excuse to turn your back on your dreams.

There is a way to free yourself from the voices that undermine you. Barbara Sher, author of *I Could Do Anything If I Only Knew What It Was*, shows the way out with a deceptively simple question, consisting of two powerful words: "Who says?"

Who says that what you really want to do isn't what you are supposed to do?

Who says that what you feel passionate about isn't practical?

Who says that trying once again to fulfill an elusive dream is a waste of time?

Who says that it's too late?

In the Tarot deck there is a card called "The Fool." The Fool is pictured as a carefree youth on a mountain path, poised to take a step forward on her journey—seemingly unaware of the fact that the step will take her right over the edge of a cliff. She has taken all her worldly possessions and put them into a small pack, which she carries lightly on her back. Her face is turned towards the sun, basking in the warmth and glow of the moment. At first glance, The Fool appears to be a simpleton. Looking at this picture, we can't help feeling superior to the youth, taking the card to be a warning against making foolish mistakes, especially when at our age, we should know better.

In fact, the card represents exactly the opposite. The Fool captures the essence of true ambition: the ability to turn your back on the voices of sensibility and reason and take the risk of listening to your own heart. The Fool doesn't settle for safety or self-protection. She wants more than coping—knowing that to cope means only to hold one's own in a battle. The Fool wants more for herself. She wants to take the risk of being fully alive.

So, who says that your greatest joy, contributions and success are not yet ahead of you? To believe this, you would have to be a fool! And that is exactly the point.

17

Ignite Your Passion

On his journey to enlightenment, a student came across a spiritual master on the road outside the village.

"Teacher, I am doing everything I can think of. I have gone to many wondrous places. I have prayed. I try to always do right and good. What else can I do?"

The wise teacher stood up and held his hands toward heaven. His fingers became like lamps of fire and he said, "If you will, you can become all flame."

If you yearn for greatness, but haven't a clue about what to try next, begin anywhere! The very act of initiating something, no matter how small or insignificant, sets forces in motion. Action brings new experiences and opportunities. If you are lost, why not begin with something you loved to do as a child? Now, take that thing up—and stay with it until you're really good at it again. You loved to play the flute. Great! Dust it off and remember how to play a favorite tune.

Enthusiasm is catching. Let the embers of your passion ignite your life and watch your greatness blaze.

18
Virtual Reality

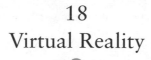

Many spiritual masters, philosophies and religions teach visualization techniques which enable you to imagine the future you want for yourself in as striking and complete detail as possible, providing an opportunity for your dreams to become manifest in the world. Abraham, who teaches through Esther Hicks, describes this as "creating a virtual reality," acting as if the future you want has already happened, feeling the unbridled joy of your positively focused thoughts.

Christiane Northrup, M.D., author of *Women's Bodies, Women's Wisdom: Creating Physical and Emotional Health and Healing*, is not what you'd traditionally call a "mystic." However, she is among those who have experimented with Abraham's notion of virtual reality, regularly expanding her ability to focus on a thought or feeling without introducing a contradicting thought or emotion. Do this for 17 seconds, Christiane has found, and "you'll see evidence of this thought manifest around you in the physical world."

So, if you've got 17 seconds to spare, go ahead right now. Close your eyes. Picture yourself in a particular scene and moment in which you are fulfilling your ambition. What are you doing? Where are you? What are you thinking? Imagine the smells, the sounds, the temperature of the air on your skin. What are you wearing? What's the expression on your face? Are there other people in the vicinity? What is their reaction to you? Just how joyful do you feel? Now imagine yourself doubling the joy! When the joy has permeated every cell of your body, go ahead and open your eyes. Prepare to be surprised!

19
Have a Plan B, C and D

————•————

Social scientists have studied individuals dealing with challenge and change in their work and lives. Their findings won't surprise you. Some people thrive no matter what comes their way. Others become victims of even the most minor setbacks. One of the key characteristics separating those who thrive from those who succumb to the pressures of life is resilience. Resilience, in this context, is not about being strong all the time. A rigid pole, set in the ground, may be equally strong from top to bottom, but when a concentrated blast of wind comes along, it will easily snap in two. There is another kind of strength in the power that comes from being flexible, bending with the ups and downs that fate sends our way.

One woman who exemplifies this quality in her work and life is Deborah Szekely, founder of Rancho La Puerta and The Golden Door, two of the world's most famous spas. Deborah's legacy of resilience can be traced to her earliest days. Her parents, who had immigrated to Brooklyn from Eastern Europe just before World War I, barely had time to catch their breath before The Great Depression reduced their food supply to bananas. In 1930, her mother gathered the family together and announced: "We're moving to Tahiti!" Her father asked: "Where's that?" To which mother replied: "I don't know, but we leave in sixteen days." The family lived out The Great Depression in their tropical paradise, living off the land.

After the Depression, Deborah returned to the U.S. where she met and married her husband, a Jewish Hungarian immigrant. At the dawn of World War II, Edmond was ordered to report for duty in the Hungarian military to fight on the side of Hitler. Seeking to evade service, they moved to Mexico as undocumented aliens. Three miles from the California border, they opened the health and fitness farm that we have come to know as Rancho La Puerta.

For many, it would be enough to have overcome these many odds, becoming one of the most famous people in one's industry. But for Deborah, this was just the beginning. She founded a second spa, The Golden Door. It became the darling of Hollywood. When the State of California exercised the right of eminent domain, putting an interstate highway right through her property, Deborah saw this as an opportunity to rebuild the facility, modeling it after a Japanese inn.

From that point on, whether by choice or by accident, Deborah has been formulating and pursuing a new dream every decade. At the age of 60, she ran for Congress. Even though she wasn't elected, she built upon her experience, and wrote a management manual for Congress, now in its eighth edition and counting. In her eighties, she is laying plans for the Immigration Museum of New Americans. "When I'm ninety, I will find another new career," she is fond of saying.

Where others would panic, certain that the future would contain only loss and heartache, Deborah faced the challenges with hope and curiosity. She never saw herself as one who set out to achieve greatness—but rather, as one who had the capacity to identify needs, and devote herself to filling them. As there will always be an abundance of needs, her optimism has never proven to be unjustified.

20
The Edge

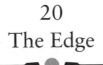

Setting goals always entails a risk: the irrational willingness to act as if things will somehow work out for you and for those for whom you care—even if you know that no matter how hard you try, how great your intentions, the outcome is quite simply not yours to call. Risk taking is no less than a summons to radical faith. It asks you to trust that there are forces at work on your behalf that are beyond your understanding and control every moment of your life.

The scholar William James explains faith by describing the novice who, upon climbing a mountain for the first time, finds himself in a situation in which the only escape is a terrifying leap across an abyss. Having had no experience with such a leap in the past, he has no basis upon which to assess his ability to survive the effort. But he notes that hope and confidence will put him in a better frame of mind for success than would fear and mistrust. James writes:

Believe, and you shall be right, for you shall save yourself;
doubt, and you shall be right, for you shall perish.
The only difference is that to believe
is greatly to your advantage.

When all the evidence seems to support your least optimistic expectations—when your past experience leads you to believe that your concerns are fully justified—it takes an almost reckless courage to have faith. But because your future is open and free, many influences will contribute to how your life will unfold over time. Ironically, your ability to hope becomes one of these factors. Perhaps it is a small consideration, but even so, it may carry just enough weight to make all the difference.

AMBITION

THE FEAR
*You are being disloyal if you put your own desires
before the needs and expectations of others.*

THE TRUTH
*The success you seek always entails a risk.
Take the behests of your own heart seriously.*

Unfinished Business

"Never," "Too late," "Can't" and "Won't:"
The language of regret
    for mistakes made, time wasted and unfulfilled dreams.
It's time for closure.
You know why—but how?
Change what you can,
Accept what you can't.
And replace words of regret,
    with wonder.

21

The Roots of Regret

When it comes to your unfinished business—unfulfilled dreams, childhood illusions exposed and not yet replaced, and mistakes gone unrectified—you probably think you have perfectly valid reasons that more than justify your regret.

- I'm too old.
- It's too late to do anything about it now.
- What's done is done.
- It won't make any difference any way.

Dig deeper, and you will see that as justified as these reasons may seem, these are simply updated versions of the same old messages that have been chasing you all the years of your life.

THE ROOTS OF REGRET

When you tell yourself: *I'm too old.*
Childhood message: *You don't have what it takes.*

When you tell yourself: *It won't make any difference, anyway.*
Childhood message: *You're insignificant and powerless.*

When you tell yourself: *I missed my chance.*
Childhood message: *You only get one try and you already blew it.*

When you tell yourself: *I had/have other priorities and responsibilities.*
Childhood message: *Your needs don't matter.*

When you tell yourself: *It's too late to do anything about it now.*
Childhood message: *You always mess things up.*

When you tell yourself: *What's done is done.*
Childhood message: *Mistakes are unfixable.*

By the sheer persistence of these messages, it would be easy for you to conclude that you are doomed to live out the rest of your days digging out from under increasingly more sophisticated versions of what your parents, teachers and other authority figures taught you about yourself and the world years ago. But aren't you sick and tired of letting their opinions run your life?

You have a choice. You can hang on to the past, whimpering into a sad, old age, citing perfectly reasonable justifications for all your unfinished business. Or you can become a truth teller, turning towards rather than away from the uncomfortable and unresolved issues in your life, reclaiming the mastery and meaning for which you yearn.

22
On Serenity

Beyond the uncomfortable and unresolved issues of your past, your destiny beckons to you to let it unfold. You have mulled and bemoaned, plotted and dreamed long enough. As the old philosopher's rule goes, while it is true that "the unexamined life is not a life worth living," it is equally true that the over-examined life "is not a life at all."

The time has come to take a stand. Face up to the tyranny of outgrown messages and beliefs and declare to the world that you matter. You have important work ahead of you to do. Only you can do it.

If there are things you need to get rid of, let them go.
If there is something you want for yourself, go get it.
If there's something you know you must do, go do it.
If you need to enlist the support of others,
    let your needs be known.
If they won't help you, go get help from someone who will.
If you lack the resources or the will,
    then accept that this is not to be.
If you accept that this is not to be,
    then surrender to life's limitations with dignity.
And after you've mourned your loss,
Accept that what is left is what is essential and true for you.
And that without this piece,
    however battered and bruised you may be,
The universe would be incomplete.

23
The Truth about Risk

*The true measure of psychological health
is just how many crises we can fit into the span of a lifetime.*
SCOTT PECK

S ome things you can change. Some things you must accept. But are you always sure which is which? Haven't we all resigned ourselves to an unpleasant situation somewhere along the road, only to discover that it would have turned out fine? Haven't we all set a goal or set out to accomplish a dream, thinking we've got what it takes to make it turn out right, only to find ourselves at a dead end? Who hasn't reached out to someone, hoping to make amends or offer forgiveness, only to be rebuffed? And then, too, haven't we all had times when we've accepted the demise of a relationship, not realizing at the time that it could have been salvaged? Why does life have to be so challenging? Because bringing your unfinished business to completion is not the cold perfection of a cut diamond, but rather, the tumultuous stuff of creation! Struggle, repent, forgive, take risks, succeed and fail, feel remorse, feel gratitude, mourn, love, and celebrate. This is the fully lived life— there is no easier way.

You are far from alone if there are times in your life when you find yourself wondering if you really have what it takes to bring closure to the wounds of the past, and fruition to all that struggles to be born. Bringing closure to the past—by changing what you can, accepting what you can't—is by its very nature a risky business. We give great lip service to the idea. But most of us are willing to take a risk only if we know that it's going to work out. The irony is, of course, that if you knew it was truly going to work out for you, it wouldn't be a risk.

In her book, *The Language of Letting Go*, Melody Beattie shares a story with us about a time she was gardening side-by-side with her mother. This was the third time Melody's plants, grown from seed, were being transferred, first from their little pot to a larger container, then transplanted into the garden and now, because Melody was moving, they were to be uprooted once again. Melody turned to her mother, a more experienced gardener, as they shook the dirt from the roots.

"Won't it hurt these plants, being uprooted and transplanted so many times?"

"Oh no," mother replied. "Transplanting doesn't hurt them. In fact, it's good for the ones that survive. That's how their roots grow strong. Their roots will grow deep, and they'll make strong plants."

Melody's mother understands that to seize the opportunities of the future we must surrender the familiarity of all that we have known—even if the pot pinched at our roots and the transition brought us face-to-face with danger.

"Won't this be hard on me?" Melody asks when confronted with the transitions in her life, feeling like one of those tender plants, turned upside down. "Wouldn't it be better if things remained the same?" Then she remembers her mother's words: "That's how the roots grow deep and strong."

Engage in life fully, and you will come to see your fate not as unknown forces in an endless void, shaking you down to your roots, but as loving hands gently guiding you home.

24

There's No Such Day as Someday

———◦●◦———

Sunny came to one of our workshops, sharing with the group that she had one piece of unfinished business that had been weighing upon her much of her life: she had always wanted to learn to play the piano. Busy raising her children and working a full-time job, she had always told herself that she'd get around to it "someday." Meanwhile, the years passed and her children had grown and were raising families of their own. Sunny pulled back on her hours at work, but now it was her declining mother, resettled in a retirement center, who was requiring more of her time and energy.

Then unexpectedly, Sunny got a phone call in the middle of the night. Her mother had passed away. Sunny told us that it had been several weeks before she felt strong enough to go back to the retirement center and handle her mother's belongings. The administrator met her at the door. "We've gone ahead and bagged up her clothes and things. But we found this under her bed." The administrator handed Sunny an old stationery box, carefully tied with a frayed pink ribbon. Sunny had never seen the box before, and yet, she sensed immediately that this was something precious to her mother, and that it would be meaningful to her, as well.

As soon as she was alone, Sunny opened the box. Inside, she found the first 79 pages of a novel, dated 1949, the year Sunny was born. Her mother had never even mentioned that she had aspirations to be a writer, let alone that she'd completed nearly 80 pages of writing so exquisite and well crafted that each word brought new tears to Sunny's eyes. Obviously, there had always been other higher priority demands upon her mother's time and resources, and the novel remained incomplete, tucked away in a box waiting for someday to arrive.

Shortly after she discovered the contents of her mother's stationery box, Sunny made a decision. She bought a piano and started taking lessons.

"You said the box had a message for you. What was it?" we asked.

Sunny looked at us and smiled.

"Simply this. There is no such day of the week called Someday."

25
Keep Current

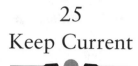

S ome things you really want to get right. When Carol's father was being wheeled away for a serious operation, she didn't think it was asking too much of life to be able to say or hear something meaningful, like "I love you," "forgive me" or "tell me why?" But somehow, in the coming and going of the orderlies and nurses, the commotion of portable machinery and buzzing fluorescent lights, the moment was lost.

You, too, may not have been able to say or hear everything you long for. Or you may realize what it is that you most want to share, ask or hear—but you think it's too late.

When you yearn to say something to someone who for any reason cannot or will not be able to hear what you want to say, there is still something you can do. Write a letter. Don't hold anything back. Say everything that's in your mind and heart, as honestly and deeply as possible.

Make room in your letter for the entire range of emotions, remembering that laughter and sadness, joy and sorrow, anger and forgiveness often come to us deeply intertwined. Don't be afraid of the emotions as they arise, grateful not only for your tears of love, but of anger and grief.

You've been let down? Of course you have. Life isn't fair? Of course it isn't. It isn't fair that good people suffer needlessly, or that bad people progress when they should be punished. Of course you are angry. Angry about your misfortunes. Angry with others who played a part. Angry with those who failed to intervene. Angry at the universe for failing to protect you from pain.

When you are done, you can keep the letter with you for as long as it takes while you decide what to do with it. Sooner or later, you will know. When you do, let it go and you will witness something unexpected. The sharp edges of incompletion and regret will begin to round and soften. Infinite grievance will turn into infinite compassion.

Gathering back your strength, you will find yourself released from the past, your gaze turned forward.

26

A Ritual for Forgiveness

————●————

The Buddhist tradition gives us a powerful ritual of forgiveness that releases us from the blame and regret we have held against others who have hurt us, others we have hurt, and transgressions we have committed against ourselves.

This forgiveness meditation was adapted from Jack Kornfield's book, *A Path with Heart*, in which Jack writes: "You will see that forgiveness is fundamentally for your own sake, a way to carry the pain of the past no longer." Begin by saying these words quietly to yourself.

FOR FORGIVENESS FROM ANOTHER

There are many ways that I have hurt and harmed you, betrayed or abandoned you, caused you suffering, knowingly or unknowingly, out of my pain, fear, anger, and confusion.

After you have spoken these words, think about the many ways and times you have hurt others. Experience the pain you caused and your own sadness and regret. When you have fully addressed each memory and sense that you are ready to release this burden, say these words:

I ask for your forgiveness.

Repeat this as often as necessary, until you have asked for forgiveness for everything that comes to mind. You are then ready for the second part of the ritual.

This time, think about all the ways you have hurt or injured yourself.

FOR FORGIVENESS FOR YOURSELF

There are many ways that I have betrayed, harmed, or abandoned myself through thought, word, or deed, knowing or unknowingly.

Feel the burden of your regret, thinking of specific times, instances, and ways you have harmed yourself. When you sense that you are ready to forgive yourself, say these words:

For each of the ways I have hurt myself, I now extend a full and heartfelt forgiveness. I forgive myself.

FOR FORGIVENESS FOR THOSE
WHO HAVE HURT OR HARMED YOU

There are many ways I have been wounded and hurt, abused and abandoned by others in thought, word, or deed, knowingly or unknowingly.

Remember these injustices, feeling the grief you have carried with you from your past. When you sense that you can release each burden, one by one, say to yourself:

In the many ways others have hurt or harmed me, whether out of fear, pain, confusion, or anger, I see these clearly now. To the extent that I am ready, I offer you forgiveness, understanding that forgiveness does not mean that I ever again will knowingly or willingly put my mind, body or spirit in harm's way. I have carried this pain in my heart too long. For this reason, to those who have caused me harm, I offer you my forgiveness and declare myself free.

27
Pass the Potatoes

S ue, one of our research participants, deeply regretted having stayed in a marriage with a man who didn't want children. Then, to make the issue even more painful, shortly after she ended her childbearing years, he left her for a younger woman. His explanation: *I wasn't ready to father a child before. Now I am.*

It was challenging enough that Sue had to come to terms with the realization that she had been betrayed on so many levels. But even worse was her mother's constant dwelling on a one-note song, that Sue had been a fool. For years, every time Sue was with her mother, she felt the sting of her judgment. She went back and forth, ricocheting between the urge to react angrily and feelings of shame that she would never be worthy of finding someone new to love.

Then somebody gave Sue a book by author Hugh Missildine. Missildine suggests that the way to break free from anger and shame is to give up trying to win approval from your disapproving parent, and to become a loving parent to yourself. When you feel the urge to lash out—at others or yourself—you, instead, tell yourself the following: "Yes, I'm really burned up, but a lot of this hate and furious resentment is simply my inner child of the past raging over past punishments I didn't deserve. But part of this is self-punishment. I am not going to fly off the handle, saying and doing things that are going to result in more punishment and hostility just to satisfy these past resentments. This isn't that much of an issue. That is the way I acted before. I do not have to be a punitive parent to myself."

Sue rehearsed this phrase many times, imagining herself visiting her mother. Then one evening, she had the opportunity to try out her new script—only to discover that the old, punitive messages had miraculously lost their sting. "I still got emotional, but something kicked in that brought me back into balance, knowing I'm really, truly okay."

Shortly thereafter, Sue decided to start dating, bracing herself to push through the fear that she was doomed to play the fool. But as she began putting out the word to her friends that she was ready to get into circulation, she realized that what had happened at dinner that night hadn't been a fluke. The old script was gone and new words had come to take its place.

"Of course I've made mistakes. But that's not the whole story about me. And what's more, it's not even the most important part," says Sue. "I laugh, I cry—and I can finally look people straight in the eye and say 'here I am, flaws and all'—the whole package. And while I prefer you love me as I am, I am willing to take the consequences."

Barbara Sher offers sage advice on how to achieve this state in the form of a vignette on the theme of hard-won self-acceptance. She suggests that you imagine yourself visiting your parents, sharing some challenging aspect of your life over dinner.

"You really screwed up," your father says sternly. Whether true or false, answer back: "Ain't it awful, Dad?" you respond with a sweet smile. "Can I have more mashed potatoes?"

Perhaps you have not achieved every one of your goals—of course you haven't. No matter who you are, time is always too short and the task always too huge. But at the same time: Isn't it true that you are a little less crazy now than you used to be? Aren't you a little more willing to tell the truth than you once were? Don't you pay a little more attention to worthwhile things? Don't you have a little more compassion for yourself and for others? And can't you find it in your heart to be a loving parent to yourself?

28
Done Apologizing

━━●━━

If you obey all the rules, you miss all the fun.
KATHERINE HEPBURN

DONE APOLOGIZING FOR...

- Not starting to save earlier for retirement
- Running out of business cards
- What kind of daughter/sister/mother/wife I've been
- How my kids are doing
- Anything I've already atoned for, whether accepted or not
- Losing touch
- What I weigh
- Watching too much TV
- Not having bought the house that has since tripled in value
- Having made foolish decisions
- A messy car or skipping a recommended tune-up
- Using the men's room when the women's line is too long
- My age (or lying about my age)
- The photo on my driver's license
- Going to bed early
- Not using coupons
- Missed opportunities
- Speaking English in foreign countries
- Anything done during my adolescent years
- Having spoiled a special occasion
- Not bringing something homemade to a potluck
- Anything that is nobody else's business
- Telling the truth (or telling a lie)
- Wanting to be the center of attention (or wanting to be left alone)
- Throwing away the bad photos of myself
- Selling somebody's gift at a garage sale
- Forgetting what I'm through apologizing for...

29
The Great Escape

━━●━━

Winnie, one of our research participants, dreamt of making "the great escape." The centerpiece of her dream was the move to a tropical island, where life would be simpler, more natural, more spiritual. Most of us recognize her dream, having a version of our own. "To move to the country." "To go around the world." "To get into an RV and just start driving."

Feeling brave and deliberately reckless, Winnie and her husband, Sam, packed their bags and headed for their island. Swept up in the excitement, they quickly found and leased a bamboo villa overlooking the ocean. The property was so inexpensive, they could put seven years worth of rent on their credit card. For weeks, Winnie gushed to us via email, attaching slide shows of the lush, tropical vistas visible from their bedroom—an open-air room bathed in sunlight and balmy breezes. There were pictures of sparkling, blue waterfalls, exotic bands of wild monkeys and picturesque palm trees laden with coconuts.

Then for a month, we heard nothing. At last, we received an email. Yes, they still loved the open vistas of the tropical landscape visible from their bed. But they hadn't counted on the fact that open walls created no degree of separation between them and the wildlife that thought of their haven as home. All night long, fat, green geckos sat on the ceiling above their bed, terrifying Winnie with their intermittent shrieks and screams. The beautiful blue waterfall entranced Winnie, until the first time it rained. Suddenly, the sparkling blue trickle of water turned into a torrent of mud. Then, there were the monkeys. Trying to get a drink from a public water fountain, Sam got too close and one of the monkeys bit him on the leg. And the final insult, a coconut fell off one of their trees and hit Winnie on the head. We're waiting for the next email, wondering if these trials were the normal tests one usually endures when crossing the threshold into the next phase of one's life—or if we would soon be asked if our guesthouse was available to rent.

In It's Only Too Late if You Don't Start Now, Barbara Sher addresses the myth of the "great escape." "Almost every day you fantasize jumping off your treadmill and making a fresh start someplace where life will be different. Everyone, especially your family, can sense your restlessness. But it's not that you want to leave them. On the contrary, you're probably trying to sell them on running away with you. You'd love to be with them in a place far beyond the reach of civilization where everything is fun again."

Barbara points out that we never visualize escaping to places we know. Rather, it's always the unknown: vague, romantic-sounding places like *the South Seas* or *the Mountains*. Just a vacation—even a long one—won't be enough for you. So desperate and extreme is your yearning, you feel that you need "something far more radical, a permanent change, cutting ties, jolting yourself awake, going far away, and making a fresh start."

And when you get there, geckos scream and monkeys bite.

But before you judge yourself as an impulsive, immature child who resents pulling an adult load, Barbara suggests that "the sense that growing up has stolen something of enormous value from you is right on target... The longing to recover your capacity for wonder comes from the side of you that was born to learn and see, to explore and question and delight in the world around you," explains Barbara. The urge to which we are responding is not so much for "place" but for the child's sense of wonder.

It is possible, although challenging, to get back to the childlike delight for which you yearn. You do so when you begin taking risks with your life again—not only in the form of grand escapes—but in the everyday opportunities that life presents to you. You imagine yourself on a tropical island, feeling the excitement and romance of watching the sun rise. But the sun rises everywhere every day, even right where you live today. When was the last time you took an unexpected break in the middle of the day, to sip a latte and read a book, just for fun? You don't need to make a great escape just to start doing yoga or to make a quilt. You regain the natural enthusiasm of your childlike wonder when you engage with life fully, taking advantage of the possibilities that arise moment by moment.

Jennifer James, in *Success is the Quality of Your Journey*, writes: "Success is every minute you live. It's the process of living. It's stopping for the moments of beauty, of pleasure; the moments of peace." The irony is that once you remember what this feels like, you don't have to get away to have the experience. You can find it anywhere.

30
The Farmer and His Horse

Once there was a farmer whose only possession of merit was a prized horse. All the people in the village ridiculed the farmer.

"Why put all your money into a horse? Somebody could steal the horse and you will have nothing."

The horse did not get stolen. But sadly, the horse did run away.

"You fool. You should never have put so many eggs in one basket. Now you have nothing. You are so unlucky."

The farmer, being a wise man, answered:

"Don't say I'm unlucky. Just say that my horse is no longer here. This is a fact. We don't know what may happen next."

Sure enough, the next day the horse returned. And with him was a pack of wild stallions.

The villagers exclaimed, "You were so right! Look how fortunate you are!"

The farmer replied, "You cannot possibly know if this is fortunate or unfortunate. We do not have the whole story yet. Merely say that we have more horses than before."

The farmer set his only son to tame the wild horses. The son was thrown and broke his leg. The doctor said he would be disabled for life.

The villagers decried his misfortune but the farmer again asked them to withhold judgment.

Soon thereafter, a war broke out in their country and all the young, healthy sons were drafted into battle. Only the farmer's son was left behind. The fighting was fierce and most of the other boys in the village died at war.

"You were right again, farmer," they said.

The farmer shouted, "On and on you go, judging this, judging that. Who do you think you are? How is it that you can presume to know how this is all going to turn out in the end?"

So it is that with this story of the farmer and his horse, the ancient Chinese philosopher Lao-tzu inspired his students to make peace with all their unfulfilled goals and ambitions.

Like the farmer's family and friends, so quick to judge according to this or that moment's results, you mourn over your dead-ends, inadequacies and mistakes, declaring yourself to have failed. But in truth, you are still in the middle of your story. It is quite simply time to stop judging yourself on the basis of your achievements and setbacks. Instead, put your faith in the adventure of your life as it unfolds. Do this and you will no longer be beating your ambition forward, trying to make the tally of your life add up. Instead, you will find your real destiny deep inside your heart, beckoning to you to let it unfold. Embark on this, the only path worth walking and regardless of your circumstances, you will always have the most supreme experience in the world: of being fully alive.

UNFINISHED BUSINESS

THE FEAR
*There are justifiable reasons why I can't do anything
about my unfinished business.*

THE TRUTH
*You've never had more knowledge and experience,
or been better equipped than today
to make peace with the past, present and future
for the best possible rest of your life.*

Love and Relationships

How we long to be loved
    by parents, siblings, lovers or mates, children and friends.
We cherish those times when love comes easily.
But how often have we been pressed by life's injustices
    to deal away broken pieces of our hearts to people
        who have neither the capacity nor desire to take our needs seriously?
Sometimes, we consume ourselves with the struggle to be loved for
    who we really are,
        other times we settle for less than we deserve
        or give up trying entirely.

There is another way:
Forgive whatever has happened in the past, the roles you and
    others have played,
        knowing that you need never put yourself in harm's way again.
Trust that just as you are, your own needs matter.
You are worthy of respect.

Take the risk of being this true to yourself, and love will
    spontaneously come to you.
Greater than any single relationship, your whole world will be filled
    with love.
And whether you are alone or with others, you will find yourself
    living in its embrace.

31

The Potential for Love

———⚫———

*When you come from love you create a force field
to which people are drawn. A loving person lives
in the center of a loving world.*

DR. DAVID VISCOTT

Donna came to one of the research circles identifying "love and relationships" as the area in which she had had the most growth.

"I had been taught from childhood that whenever there was a conflict between what I wanted and my husband's desires, it was the wife's obligation to give way. I knew that I was unhappy for a fair portion of our thirty years together, but I didn't have the courage or strength to do anything about it."

Then, after the kids were grown, John had an affair with a business associate. "It would probably have devastated me—but the truth is, by ignoring my own needs and interests for so many years, I had pretty much already devastated myself."

Shortly thereafter, a friend introduced Donna to the work of David Viscott, M.D., whose teachings about love and relationships inspired her to rethink her life.

"A relationship has to have the potential for loving," she heard him say on his tape, *Discovering the Love You Have to Give.* "If you have to hold back some part of yourself in a relationship with the person you love, then you are withholding a part of yourself that should be loved, and you are always wishing for that part to be loved... It's wonderful to be with someone where you can cross the threshold at night, and you know that it's safe because no matter what you say or do, it's going to be accepted."

Following the lecture, Donna made a concerted attempt to forgive her husband his infidelity while vowing to give voice to the long neglected parts of herself. It turned out, as she had feared, that John liked the "new Donna" less than the "old Donna," and the straws of their marriage scattered to the wind. As soon as the divorce papers were signed, she did something completely out of character: booking herself on a singles cruise to Mexico.

"It was such a daring act. But once on board, I could see that once again, I was going to have to deal with others' expectations. As much as I wanted to find new love, I wasn't sure I was willing to pay such a steep price ever again. I remember sitting in a corner of the ballroom with tears in my eyes when Samuel asked me to dance."

Donna turned him down, but he didn't walk away. In fact, he offered his ear and a handkerchief.

"Instantly, I got it. Here was someone who was going to let me be myself. I could cry, I could whine, I could be angry and not have to worry about what anyone thinks. He wasn't even trying to cheer me up. He just sat with me quietly, letting me be."

For Donna, that turned out to be the secret of finally experiencing the unconditional love for which she'd yearned.

In the words of Dr. Viscott: "If you owe anything to yourself, it's to let yourself alone."

32

Name Your Relationship

——•——

Every relationship has its own, unique name. Some relationships are "Love," some are "Compassion," some are "Best Friends." Even difficult relationships have provided opportunities for you to develop qualities you might not otherwise have developed in your life: "Patience," "Righteous Anger," or "Justice," among the possibilities. Each one of these qualities is a shorthand way to think about the positive role even a difficult relationship can play in your life.

So think about a relationship you'd like to heal or celebrate right now, and honor it with a name.

33

If Not Now, When?

———•———

When we daydream about our relationships, we envision ourselves as being loved fully, our needs and desires taken seriously by others. Out of abundance, we can imagine ourselves giving freely and generously to those for whom we care.

In the meanwhile, we have issues. We give too much and feel unappreciated. We place our faith in others and are disappointed. We make demands that are unmet, hold grudges and shut down to self-protect. Sometimes, our issues are so powerful, they can't be overcome by the physical separation of distance and even death.

However can we get from our issues, past and present, to the abundant and loving future we envision for ourselves?

Here's a simple exercise that will show you the way. But be forewarned: it may be simple, but it won't be easy.

Pick a relationship that is on your mind right now, past or present—one that is in some important way unresolved. Now recall a specific incident that exemplifies your dissatisfaction. Recreate it in your imagination with as much detail as possible. Where are you? What happened? If there is dialogue, is what you are saying the same as what you are thinking? If not, why not? How are you feeling? What is the expression on your face? How does your body feel?

Now what about the other actor in this scene? What role is he or she playing in your memory? Is there mutual respect? Do your needs matter? How do you wish things could be different and what stops you from changing what you can, accepting what you can't?

Now, ten years have passed and nothing has been resolved. You still have the same issues and you still hold the same positions. How do you look now? How do you feel? How do you wish things could be different and what stops you from changing what you can, accepting what you can't?

Finally, imagine yourself approaching the end of your life, this relationship still unresolved. What is the expression on your face? How do you feel about how you have handled this relationship? Do you see yourself being loved fully, your needs and desires taken seriously? Do you imagine yourself giving freely and generously to those for whom you care? If not, take out pen and paper and from the perspective of these advanced years, write a letter to yourself at your current age, giving yourself the most loving advice you can, responding to these two questions:

1. What do you know you need to be doing differently to get the best possible outcome?

2. If not now, when?

34
Say "Yes" to the Facts

——●——

Some time ago, Carla found herself complaining bitterly to her friend Lisha about a failed partnership. She had held high expectations for the venture, bringing her best intentions to the relationship. When disagreements arose between them that could not be overcome, she was understandably distressed.

"What went wrong?" Lisha asked.

"I don't know. Maybe I didn't give enough. Maybe I should have overlooked more. Maybe I should have tried harder," Carla responded.

"That's sad," Lisha replied. "It's bad enough when you bring your best to a situation and the world says 'no' to you—but it's twice as bad when you find yourself saying 'no' to yourself."

Lisha's words stayed with Carla. She realized that she had grown up in a family dynamic that often made demands upon her to deny her own voice in order to avoid "rocking the boat." While she found many ways to dance with and around a long list of "shoulds" and "oughts," Carla was well-trained to stop just shy of crossing the line that would have simultaneously offered both the pain of separation and the promise of freedom. By the time the last of her parents died, she was ready to free herself from the enmeshed family relationships that had kept her in an ongoing state of apology. But as Lisha astutely pointed out to her, her lifetime of compromises had left Carla lacking a critical skill: the ability to say "yes" to her own point of view.

Many of us grew up in families where our survival depended on interpreting facts from other players' points of view. But the truth is that only you can judge if your own intentions are well-meaning, if you do your fair share, if your demands are reasonable, if your mistakes or shortcomings are outweighed by the good that you do No matter how others may interpret the facts and put their own spin on you, you have the right to take your own side on your own behalf! Stop congratulating yourself for violating your honest needs, interests and opinions in the name of compassion, an attempt to understand, or the urge for self-improvement. Believe in yourself and stop apologizing for thinking, saying and acting on what is true for you.

The next time Carla had lunch with Lisha, her friend asked if she had recovered from the partnership break-up. Lisha braced herself for another long list of shoulda's and coulda's. Rather, she found herself applauding the elegance of Carla's simple but hard-won response: "I'm just sad it didn't work out."

Author Oriah Mountain Dreamer captures the essence of this leap to freedom in these lines from her prose poem.

THE INVITATION
It doesn't interest me if the story you are telling me is true.
I want to know if you can disappoint another to be true
  to yourself...
I want to know if you can live with failure, yours and mine,
  and still stand on the edge of the lake and shout to the silver
  of the full moon,
"YES."

35
The Way to Cross the Chasm

————●————

The elderly rabbi felt compelled to undertake a perilous journey in order to do a good deed in the mountainous terrain beyond the gates of the village. He journeyed for many days and at last approached his destination, a shepherd's hut in which an old friend lay dying. But between him and the hut stretched a seemingly bottomless chasm. The rains had washed away the simple bridge the shepherd's family once so joyously traversed. And so, the rabbi asked God what to do.

Immediately, his eyes fell upon the trunk of a fallen tree. While it would easily stretch across the chasm, it was very narrow and unstable. With great effort, the rabbi managed to swing the log into place, securing it as best he could. Praying that it would hold, he inched his way forward step by step, finally making it across to the little hut. And after he had done his good deed, he made it back again in the same manner.

When he returned to his village, he told his students about what had transpired.

"Rabbi," one asked. "The bridge was so unsteady. How could you ever have made it across the chasm?"

"How did I manage?" the rabbi replied. "Simply this. When I felt myself toppling to one side, I leaned to the other."

So it is with your own journey. You can make progress toward what you want simply by counteracting your excesses. If you have a tendency to say no, try saying yes. If you always lean towards compliance, balance this tendency with resistance. If you have been passive, try taking action. If you have been in a frenzy, try calming down.

If you tend to blame yourself for things, seek to recognize those aspects for which you bear no responsibility. If you feel that you are never to blame, see what is possible for you to correct.

Get the balance right with yourself, and you, too, will progress.

36
Love Your Way Out: A Checklist

—◆●◆—

How can we be so smart about so many aspects of our lives—and yet have such a terrible time ending outgrown relationships? We know it is damaging to stay in toxic or abusive relationships and yet we do everything we can to avoid the final goodbye and when we do find a way to move on, there is often bloodshed.

But ending something bad, wrong, unfortunate or just plain foolish doesn't mean that you have to inflict a mortal wound upon yourself, or another. Instead, when you recognize that a relationship is no longer working for you, the best way to move forward is simply this: to love your way out of it.

Based on the collective wisdom of such teachers as Unity minister Karen Boland, Melody Beattie in her book, *The Language of Letting Go*, and Abraham teaching through Esther Hicks, we have prepared *Love Your Way Out: A Checklist*. Consult this list if you yearn to leave an outgrown relationship behind and are looking for the best way to do so.

LOVE YOUR WAY OUT: A CHECKLIST
In regard to ending an outgrown relationship...

1. Have I taken the time to recall the positive things between us, knowing all the while that acknowledging these particular qualities and characteristics does not necessarily mean that it is right or necessary for me to stay in this relationship with you?

2. Do I have the wisdom and courage to admit that sabotaging the relationship, manipulating you to end it or letting it fade away through attrition—all misguided attempts to "spare your feelings"—only seem to be easier roads to ending a relationship but, in fact, inflict maximum damage on us all?

3. Recalling the love that we have shared, even if our relationship needs to end, have I communicated my feelings, my wants and my intentions honestly, directly and definitively to you, hoping that I will be heard, but not depending upon it?

4. In rejecting the negative aspects of this relationship, have I also examined and rejected the negative messages that were embedded in it, such as "all relationships are flawed" or "I'll never find the right person?"

5. Do I recognize that the damage done to me by holding onto anger and resentment far outweighs the satisfaction of justifying to myself and others that I am right about ending this, especially since no justification to others is necessary?

6. What have I learned from this experience that I no longer have to repeat, having already demonstrated my mastery of the lessons that this relationship held for me by my willingness to let you go?

7. Am I eager and willing to take my attention off of what has gone wrong in the past and onto what it is I want more of in my life?

8. Can I forgive you as well as myself, trusting that by generously walking away in a spirit of peace and love, I will be in the best position possible to attract these qualities into my life in the future?

You will know that you have satisfactorily completed your checklist when you think about your outgrown relationship without feeling bitter, angry, hurt or upset.

Do this and you will have closure on the past, making room for the experience of the love for which you yearn. It will come to you in ways both unexpected and new.

37
Piece Your Life Together

━━ ●━ ━━

For many nights, Marilyn stood a lonely vigil at her mother's hospital bed in the intensive care unit. Lapsed into a semi-comatose state, her mother could neither see nor hear and her words were unintelligible. There was no one but Marilyn there to witness what happened on the final night when suddenly, her mother's eyes opened wide and she cried out: "I love you Sondra" and then fell silent. "It's not Sondra, Mom. It's me: Marilyn" she cried out, but mother was already gone.

Sondra was Marilyn's sister, always the favorite—and now, with her mother's dying breath, Marilyn knew, with a terrible finality, that she was doomed to have a mother-shaped hole in her heart forever.

The research circle listened to Marilyn's story, paying rapt attention to each and every word, for each of us had also relinquished painfully shaped pieces of our hearts to the injustices of life. Marriages that had failed, children unborn or gone astray, siblings disowned. But as we listened, the most interesting thing was this: just two years after this painful episode, Marilyn looked fine. She looked more than fine. In fact, she could tell us her story, all the while looking completely at peace.

"All your life, you yearned for something that was never to be yours," one of us inquired. "How did you make things right with yourself after that?"

"Before I knew how this chapter in my life story would end, I had kept the space where the love was supposed to be empty, waiting in a state of ongoing yearning and hope. I was like a broken pot, the structure weakened by what I now know definitively was an illusion. The sad tale over at last, I realized that if I ever wanted to be whole and strong, I would have to fill that empty place up with something else."

Of course she mourned her terrible loss, but before long, she realized that by giving up the dream, she had also been freed. Her life had blossomed, full of friends, family and the best company of all: her own, healed self.

The image Marilyn shared reminded us of the mended pots from archeological digs on display in museums around the world. Here there would be a lyrical etching of dancing girls holding hands around the middle of an earthen pot's bulging belly. There, where a leg had once tapped out its rhythmic steps, would be a seamlessly crafted patch of white. The pieced together pot now stands renewed, ready to face the ages, even stronger at the mended places than the original.

Piecing together your own broken pot of dreams, you will come to understand that the depth of your yearning is merely an indication of the enormity of your capacity for love. Once you stop investing all your energy in trying to find the missing piece, you will discover that you already have the whole world in your heart.

38

A Question of Containment

—◖●◗—

W hen life is unjust, it is logical for you to make the move to self-protect. Hurriedly, you throw up a wall around your wounded spirit. Caring for yourself deeply, you take whatever measures are necessary to defend the vulnerability of your fragile soul.

But what if you are mistaken?

What if rather than weak and broken, your soul is strong and your spirit indomitable?

Of course it is always wise to put distance between yourself and those who cannot be trusted with more than they can handle responsibly.

But rather than thinking of self-protective walls as boundaries, think of them as containers for your vital spirit. Then, rather than reacting against hostile forces that have the power to threaten your essence, you can choose if, how and when to allow others to participate in your life, to share in the truth, beauty, strength and goodness of who you really are.

39
The Photo Pledge

———•———

Set aside time to go through an album of childhood photographs of yourself. Make this a special experience, finding a comfortable place where you can be alone and undisturbed.

When you are settled in, look closely at the pictures of yourself in the album, searching for a photo that expresses how you were feeling at the time. Look at the expression in your eyes and around your mouth, in particular. How about body posture?

Once you have found a photo that speaks to you, write a pledge to that child in the photo. Make a promise to her that you will do everything in your power to reclaim all that was hidden deep in her heart. Promise that you will do the hard emotional work of retrieving her authentic self, derailing self-defeating patterns, healing the pain and saying yes to love.

40
Whose Turn Is It?

S he was already in her seventies when she met the man of her dreams. All of her life she had longed for such perfection. For ten amazing years, they lived together. Every day was a blessing, full of love and light. And then she died.

Standing before the angel who awaited her at the gate to heaven, she begged for an explanation.

"Why couldn't you have sent him to me earlier?" she cried. "When I think of how many men I tried to love, with so little in return. And then to get it all—but so late! Why did I have to wait so long?"

The angel replied. "In your twenties, you knew exactly what you wanted out of life. You chose Mark and it didn't work out.

"When you were in your thirties and forties, you thought you knew what would make you happy. You chose Stan and it didn't work out.

"When you were in your fifties and sixties, you believed you had learned from your experiences and that now you knew what was right for you. You chose Martin and it didn't work out.

"In your seventies, you realized you didn't have a clue and gave up."

"Yes, that's true," the woman replied. "And then after that, I met Carl and had the happiest years of my life. But that still doesn't answer my question. Why did it take so long?"

"That's easy," replied the angel. "I was waiting for you to finish taking your turn."

LOVE AND RELATIONSHIPS

THE FEAR
You are not worthy of respect.
Your needs don't matter.

THE TRUTH
Say yes to yourself, and whether you are alone or with others,
you will find yourself living in love's embrace.

Parenting Grown Children

For decades, you guide, brood over and protect your children,
　　encircling them with love, celebrating their accomplishments,
　　remedying their deficits.

But sooner or later, your children outgrow the embrace of even your
　　best advice,
　　and for better and sometimes for worse, strive to become a
　　center of their own.

There will be those times when you find it hard to love them
　　without pain,
　　discovering that by asking you to truly let them go,
　　life is making demands upon you greater than any of us
　　should have to endure.

There is a way to make it through, however, but it won't be easy
　　for you:
For you must become willing to replace concern with interest
　　in your children's lives,
　　to trade your agendas for them with acceptance,
　　to sacrifice the way things were in order to give them
　　the space to grow,
　　and to cultivate a new center of your own.

Do this, and you will experience the most precious of loves—
　　an understanding that transcends all that has come before:
　　to be able to laugh and cry,
　　to be whole in your grown child's presence,
　　and to trust that this is enough.

41

The Cards We're Dealt

Four old friends who had shared the same card table for many years gathered together for one of their favorite pastimes: a game of bridge. As the story goes, as soon as the cards were dealt, silence filled the room. Finally, one of the women issued a long, heartfelt "Oy vey."

Without skipping a beat, the second woman also sighed: "Oy vey."

Then, the third woman joined in with her own: "Oy vey."

Finally, the fourth woman looked around the table, and replied: "I thought we all agreed not to speak about our children."

42
What Did You Do?

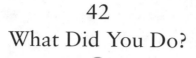

For all of us, there comes a moment when we look at our adult children and worry. Your grown son has dropped out of school? Your daughter is on her second divorce? You still get calls for money—or you never get calls from your children at all?

In the late hours of the night, you feel guilty for a spectrum of omissions and commissions: You didn't love them enough; you loved too much; you were too strict; you were too permissive. The list goes on and on. You ask yourself what you did or didn't do to have unwittingly caused harm to the very ones you most hoped to protect.

The answers come easily enough. But you are asking the wrong question. What you really should be asking yourself is not *"What did I do?"* but rather, *"What did I do when I was their age?"*

Ah hah! See how the clouds of self-judgment part and you suddenly remember what it's like to be 18 or 27 or 42? Do you remember when you thought you could chart an easier/happier/more efficient path through life, only to discover that your shortcut led straight to disappointment? Did you take risks/experiment/act or think out-of-the-box, only to come to regret your decisions? Or did you strive to be perfect, dutifully following all the rules, coming up short, anyway? Did you have to grapple with consequences, apologize, reconsider, regroup and retool when you were your adult child's age, give or take a year or two?

The truth is that we all stumble through life—sometimes in a state of confusion, at other times in a state of grace. Take a good look around, and you will soon come to realize that even if things aren't perfect, they're not the worst they could be, either. That we advance at all—that we learn from our mistakes, dust ourselves off to try again, find it in our hearts to take a risk yet again and even, from time to time, discover that we can somehow, despite ourselves, luck into something good—is life's miracle.

That our children can do the same is more than a miracle—it's to be expected.

So drop the judgment—of yourself as well as of them—and get some sleep.

43

Set Aside Your Agenda

——•——

Your children don't want your advice. Have you noticed? We're not saying that there might not be times when your adult child comes to you and asks your opinion about something. But there is something deep, important, healthy in them that pushes you out of the center of their lives just when it seems to you that the stakes are highest, the potential for mistakes the greatest. We know that we can spare them so much pain. We want to give them our experience, our wisdom, our perspective. But in the words of author and psychologist Scott Peck, they may "want our admiration and gifts and money, but they don't want us."

Peck describes the wrenching experience of a loving parent faced with negotiating a new relationship with his or her adult children. "There comes a time, gradually or suddenly, subtly or dramatically, when we need to step aside," he writes. "It's impossible to know how to do it right. Children are likely to blame us for doing it too soon or too abruptly. They are unlikely to have any appreciation for how difficult it may be for the parent to dramatically change roles. But so what? It's not an issue of ease. It's simply what needs to be done."

In our experience, even if you vow to surrender control, remembering to withhold unasked-for advice, our children sense our judgment, as long as there is even a hint of concern left in us. The truth is, as long as you want your offspring to make good choices, to live up to their potential or even, for heaven's sake, simply to be happy, they will do their best to buck you off their saddle.

So what's the alternative? Dr. David Viscott teaches that recovery begins the moment you feel free to look your adult offspring in the eye, and know, deep in your gut, that it's no longer your job to make them feel better. "Make your world a place where a child can sit down with you in the kitchen and say, 'You know what?' And you say, 'What?' He starts talking and is saying things about being unhappy—and you try to talk him out of being unhappy! No, don't try to talk him out of it. He's unhappy. You must allow him to be unhappy."

No agendas, no solutions, no answers. Just a hot cup of coffee and a place where your children can be real, and perhaps someday, when they have calmed down enough to realize that there is somebody else in the room with issues of her own, they can return the favor to you.

44

A Parent's Prayer

———■●■———

O ur friend Agnes lives next door to her daughter, her daughter's husband and her two grandchildren. With our own children scattered across the country, we have to admit that we are sometimes jealous of how close they are. They go shopping together. They frequently dine at each other's houses. The grandchildren drop in spontaneously day and night. But over a rare pot of tea, Agnes admitted to us that she isn't so sure that closeness with one's adult children is such a blessing.

"I wanted to live near Gwen and the kids. But somewhere along the line, I realized that a side-product of this level of intimacy is, simply put: *I know too much about them.* Between the four of them, not to mention my son and his family and my husband's and my own issues, there's always something wrong with someone, somewhere consuming me."

Agnes paused. When she spoke again, it was with a poignant tone.

"You know, when I think about my grandmother, Molly, she had a better handle on this than do I. You see, she had nine children and 25 grandchildren, and she couldn't possibly invest the level of worrying into each one that I bring to the table. For her, it was enough to know that her children weren't sick or in jail. Short of that, they had to fend for themselves. Perhaps it's better that way."

Identifying with Agnes's yearning for peace of mind, we recognize that between e-mail, phones and cheap airfare, our adult children don't have to live next door for us to know just enough to be consumed with worry.

Who doesn't wish we could protect our children and our children's children all their lives? But life's unknowns have a way of sometimes spinning circumstances out of our control. Even Agnes's grandmother, Molly, made exceptions for her nine children and 25 grandchildren when a genuine crisis was at hand.

In the meanwhile, she was always ready to listen to them, cry with them and serve up a hot cup of soup. And one more thing, Agnes reports. "She prayed a lot."

Here is Molly's favorite prayer.

MOLLY'S PRAYER

God—Here's my family, and here are all our worries.
I've done what I can. Now, it's your turn.
Amen.

45
Solving the Riddle

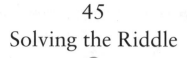

You're just being yourself when suddenly, Tanya, your adult daughter, looks at you with total disdain. Perhaps what engaged your child's wrath is something as simple as your refusal to send your burned steak back to the restaurant kitchen. You have no idea why your decision to keep quiet about the blackened meat merits such a big, negative response.

So, here's a clue. What your children like least about you is what they most want to change about themselves.

In poetic words credited to psychoanalyst Margaret Mahler, it is as though in the parade of generations, children are given both roots and wings. The roots ground them in their family's data bank, giving them a sense of belonging and a place from which to move out into the world. The wings provide them with the means to autonomy—the ability to advance their family's personal histories and try for something better.

You may recall the sixth insight in James Redfield's book, *The Celestine Prophecy*. Many of us read it while our nests were still occupied. His insight is that each one of us represents the next step of evolution along the lineage created by our two parents. "Our higher purpose on earth can be found by recognizing what our parents accomplished and where they left off," Redfield writes.

Viewed from this perspective, you may be able to see your adult child's disdain not as a random, isolated incident, but as a continuum in the evolutionary progression from generation to generation. Following is our adaptation of Redfield's insight:

1. Describe your mother, her attitude towards her family and her accomplishments. Think of positive and negative words that describe your mother's personality, paying particular attention to her worst traits. Now, think about your mother's childhood. In what way did her childhood environment and experiences

influence her stances and choices in life? Now, summarize your mother's underlying belief about life in as few words as possible. Finally, ask yourself: what was missing from your mother's life, and what have you done in your life to address this deficit?

2. Now, describe your father in terms of his attitude towards his family and his accomplishments. Think of positive and negative words that describe your father's personality, paying particular attention to his worst traits. Now, think about your father's childhood. In what way did his childhood environment and experiences influence his stances and choices in life? Now, summarize your father's underlying belief about life in as few words as possible. Finally, ask yourself: what was most missing from your father's life, and what have you done in your life to address this deficit?

3. In trying to resolve the issues and discrepancies between your parents' philosophies and deficits, what life question emerged that was uniquely yours to answer? What part of this have you successfully addressed? What more is there to do?

And now, here's the million-dollar question:
4. In what ways, does your child's negative response to you address the unresolved elements of your own and your spouse's life questions? Chances are that this has become your child's own life question.

In the case of Tanya, angry over her mother's refusal to send back the overdone steak, the daughter was subconsciously working out the unfinished business of her family's dynamics: a strong and strict father who bossed his wife and children around, and a loving but ineffectual mother who had trouble standing up for her and her offspring's rights. The daughter's life question was this: *how can I be both loving and warm (like my mother) while finding the strength (like my father) to stand up for what's right?* Ergo: the larger than life importance of the inflammatory steak.

Having figured this out, next time you may have more understanding about the source of your child's disdain—and even, in some secret depths of your soul—find it in your heart to cheer your offspring on. And while it is probably best for you to keep your astute analysis to yourself, knowing this, you may yet somehow find yourself demanding properly cooked steaks in the future.

46
Schedule a Yard Sale

— ● —

I t's easier to accept that the time has come to let go of our adult child than it is to actually do it. We miss the fun times we had playing, learning, loving together as a young family. We are reluctant to relinquish our roles as champion and protector, cheerleader and nurse. And, of course, above all, because we still love our child, we wish there were more time to rectify the mistakes we made, realizing that to let go now means that our child's issues are no longer ours to fix.

All this is true. Still, it's time to let go to make space for all that is to come. So, what are the old beliefs, the stresses, the regrets that no longer serve you or your child? Look around your house and take the reminders of these things that you and your child have outgrown and put them in a yard-sale pile.

- Find something that represents the expectations and unfulfilled dreams you once had for your child, and for your own role as mother to this child, that you would be willing to let go. How about the yellowing folder of piano sheet music that you'd hoped would start your child on a concert career—but your offspring preferred football? Start your pile.

- Now, what can you find around the house that reminds you of the consuming stresses and obligations you carried as a mother to this child? Relinquishing it symbolizes your newfound freedom to reclaim your passion, to create anew. Put it in the pile.

- What can you find that reminds you of the sadness surrounding the erroneous belief that being a loving mother to this child was supposed to have been enough forever? Put it in the pile.

- What can you put up for sale that will carry away with it any of the regrets you may have about how you raised your child, remembering—of course—that you did good things as a parent, too? Put it in the pile.

Letting go means you'll miss many parts of the past, but it's going to be alright because this is healthy and natural and the way it was always meant to be. As each item makes its way out of your yard and to someone else's home, set it free with a blessing. *I honor the past, I welcome the future.*

47
The Dance

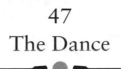

Rebecca, 24, married a fundamentalist who believed that it was his God-given mission to convert not only Rebecca, but also her mother to his faith.

Simon was upset because at age 35, his mother has asked him to move out of the house.

Sylvia, 19, had a child on her own, and then stopped talking to her mother when she refused to raise the child for her.

Several years later, all three mothers had established acceptable, if not ideal, relationships with their offspring. How? By learning the dance.

The dance goes like this. Rebecca sashays in at her husband's side. Simon steps on his mother's toe. Sylvia twirls her mother back around. Mothers back off and swinging low they argue, they struggle or don't talk to their children at all for a whole year.

After taking a break, mothers and offspring realize that despite the ups and downs, the dance of love and connection is not yet through. They learn to sashay around the parts of each other's lives they simply cannot embrace and love the rest. Rebecca and her mother now have a tacit agreement not to talk about religion but they still have a great time shopping together on a weekday afternoon. Simon was angry for a year after his parents forced him to move out. For a while, he slept on the couch of a friend's house. But eventually, he found a studio apartment not far from home—and while his mother wishes that Simon would do his own laundry—they are both free, at last, to live their separate lives. Sylvia found a roommate with a baby of her own. They take turns watching each other's child and share expenses to make their complicated but rewarding lives work. Her mother finally gets to be the grandmother she'd always dreamt of being—generous and loving, but with boundaries intact.

So that's the dance—a few steps forward, a few steps back...and in the end, with a little bit of luck and a lot of hard, emotional work, a curtsy and a bow.

48
The Last Bird

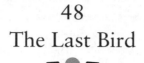

J ust now, as the sadness of separation begins to turn from fog to mist, you can catch glimpses of your own future freedom beckoning to you. "You have given so much for so long," your future calls to you. "So often, you put your children's needs before your own. You sacrificed so much of your own creativity in fair trade for the joy of helping others reach their potential. And now it is time for you to take back your own time—to make choices that play out the fulfillment of your own emotional, intellectual and creative destiny."

You are, in fact, on the verge of discovering what is no less than what author Barbara Sher calls "your second life."

"Your first life belongs to nature," she explains. "Your second life belongs to you. What's coming is a gradual loosening of the hold that culture and biology have on you, and the arrival of your authentic self. You're moving into a life that's sure to be more conscious, centered, creative, and energetic than anything you've known so far."

In this, your second life, no longer is it selfish to tend to your own needs and interests first. "You can forget until midlife that only part of you is a provider and a parent; the other half of you is just you," says Barbara. "It's not that you should have run your life differently; we all need to take up responsibilities at a certain age, to love and care for people besides ourselves, or to build our careers. But one day, it's time to give up some of those long-time responsibilities and begin a second life."

In the beginning this newfound freedom may feel uncomfortable. You may take refuge in the familiarity of thinking of others first. You may even worry that investing in yourself is somehow taking away from your children's potential for success. But, in fact, the greatest gift you can give your adult children is to get on with living your own happy life.

49

The New Rules of Engagement

Ten rules to consider in establishing a healthy adult relationship with your offspring:

1. If you are tempted to offer advice or deliver an opinion about something they are considering doing/facing, Stop! Think: have you specifically been asked? Is it a matter of life and death? If not, better to keep your thoughts to yourself.

2. If your child asks you for money, if you give it at all, give it only if you can part with it freely, with neither emotional nor practical strings, expectations or paybacks attached. And, too, keep the next rule in mind:

3. Never do for them what they can (or ought to be able to) do for themselves.

4. The only possible exception to this is paying for their health insurance for at least awhile, since young adults think they're immortal.

5. Other than that, be willing to let them fail and figure out how to get themselves out of messes. That's the only way they'll learn.

6. Listen to their complaints about what you did or didn't do to them during their childhoods without letting yourself (or them) get caught up in the drama. (Know, by the way, that you did your best, that it is the human condition to fall short of expectations somewhere/somehow, that every life has challenges to be overcome, and that one heartfelt apology should suffice.)

7. Keep your visits short and fill them with fun things and good food.

8. Find something, somewhere in your life that unlike your adult child, is still under your control, and master it.

9. Remember that you've got the right to break old patterns, establish healthy boundaries and raise the bar in terms of how you deserve to be treated, regardless of what dysfunctions and dramas are playing out in your offspring's life.

10. Keep breathing. It's going to be okay.

50
Loving Words

The most freeing thing a parent can say to an adult child are these empowering words that Jimmy's father gave to her:

"You're so smart. You know just what to do."

PARENTING GROWN CHILDREN

THE FEAR
*A woman's worth is measured by other people's opinions
about the success of her child.*

THE TRUTH
*The greatest gift you can give your adult children
is to get on with living your own happy life.*

Beauty

Don't bother complimenting us about how we must have been such
  beauties when we were younger—
  or that we look so good for our age now.

For our looks, at last, are our own business—
  —To decorate with wild abandon to express our creativity or
  —To cultivate organically to send roots down deep or
  —To veil with invisibility in order to enjoy the freedom of living
    off the grid or
  —Some of all of these and more, if that's what we please.

So forgive us for being too busy to notice who or what you think
  we are,
As we celebrate the certainty that our natural beauty has grown
  proportionately
  to the exact degree that our hearts have become open and free.

51

The Gifts of Your Ancestors

ow would your great grandmother have looked if she had lived to be your age? Take a moment to imagine yourself being her at your age, sensing how it feels to live, work and move around in her body. What were her attitudes about style, cosmetics and personal appearance? About nutrition and weight? About beauty, in general?

When Jimmy visualized herself as her great grandmother, she saw herself bent over a hoe, working the soil of the family farm somewhere in rural Kentucky. "At most, I used a strong bar of soap and wore a loose dress shaped out of tough cotton I'd made for myself years ago. My gray hair was tied back in a knot and my skin was dried into deep lines from long hours in the sun. Imagining my great grandmother's posture and spirit, I felt and looked much older than I do today at the exact same age. At the same time, I recognized the determination in her eyes and saw the inner strength of her own special beauty: a quality she most probably neglected to appreciate about herself but that I am eager to emulate."

After you imagine yourself as your great grandmother, repeat the process, this time thinking first about your grandmother and then your mother. If you are fortunate enough to have photographs of the generations of women who came before you when they were your age, take the time to study them, letting the expressions on their faces, their clothes, their posture tell their own unique stories—the convergence of physical inheritance with time, place, circumstances and attitudes.

Now it is time to look into the mirror and read your own story about beauty, seeking first to appreciate qualities about yourself that transcend time and place. Similarities in eye color, perhaps, a certain curve to your hips or an inner strength indicated by the set of your jaw. Take a moment to appreciate this legacy of the relationship to beauty that is yours: echoes of the past that continue to impact how you feel about yourself, here and now.

But how, too, are things different for you than those who came before? No matter how much you may identify with them, yours is a chapter about beauty that is still being written. So look into the mirror and ask yourself: *What is my story about beauty going to be—a story unique to my own time, place and circumstances?* And knowing that you get to write your story for yourself, ask yourself this as well: *Just how original, surprising and wonderful would I like it to be?*

52
The Continuum

———◦———

Two good friends were on the same page about so many issues, they took it for granted that no major rifts were ever likely to develop between them. Then, on her 55th birthday, Linda announced that she was going gray, believing it to be dishonest to continue coloring one's hair at her age. Joan agreed.

Linda's hair grew in a gorgeous rich steel gray.

Joan's hair, on the other hand, was a lifeless, washed-out brown. Before long, despite feeling she was somehow betraying her friend, Joan quietly put her hair back on the bottle. It was not a subject the two ever discussed.

On her 56th birthday, Joan remarked off-handedly to Linda, "I would never have work done on my face. You can always tell who's had work, it looks so unnatural."

Joan had great skin.

Linda did not. In fact, Linda was mortified to admit to her friend that she had scheduled a facelift for herself. The relationship survived—but barely.

Ask a group of women to compare and rate the different approaches to appearance taken by, say, a Barbara Bush versus a Suzanne Somers. One, you will hear, is "letting herself go." The other, you will hear, is embarrassing herself by "pretending to be something she is not." All manner of moral, psychological, political and social implications will be attached to these most personal of decisions about how we choose to show up in life.

So here's what we think. We think judgments about nipping and tucking, hair color and hormones, plumping out or dieting, and so on and on, are none of each other's business. As always, marketers in a wide range of industries have a vested interest in pitting women against one another because, God forbid, we should just be happy with our own choices and let others have theirs. In case you've forgotten, here's a quick refresher course on what Naomi Wolf wrote in her book, *The Beauty Myth*, over a decade ago. "I argue that we deserve the choice to do whatever we want with our faces and bodies without being punished by an ideology that is using attitudes, economic pressure, and even legal judgments regarding women's appearance to undermine us psychologically and politically."

If we aren't willing to be divided up into mutually exclusive boxes, how can we get a handle on how and where we fit into the bigger picture? The answer is the continuum. We're all on it. A vast array of overlapping choices, with as many combinations of possibilities as there are women in our generation. Barbara Bush may be at one end and Suzanne Somers on the other—but we are all making decisions and taking actions that impact how we present ourselves to the world all the time. Is it okay to spend money on moisturizer but not to have your eyes done? Is it okay to have your eyes done but not okay to have a facelift? These are personal preference issues—not moral ones. Choosing to proceed with any particular service or adornment does not make you an imposter—and choosing to refrain does not mean you aren't making intelligent, appropriate and sometimes even courageous decisions about who you are and where you are on the continuum at this point of your life, either.

Like all the women of our generation, dealing with your appearance is one of many issues to be addressed. On any given day, you may find yourself struggling to set and make your goals. You may be making decisions or you may be changing your mind; you may be feeling gratitude or you may be mourning losses; you may be getting up again and trying something new. This is where the juice is. More important than being beautiful: being fully, radiantly, gorgeously alive.

53
Gathering Style

Lori came to one of our research circles, sharing with the group that she felt more attractive today than when she was in her thirties, several decades ago. Her features haven't changed much. If anything, she'd put on a few pounds. But, if you were to ask us what it is about Lori that allows her to radiate such effortless beauty, we would have to sum it up in one word: style.

After the session, we made a date to take a walk with Lori through a forest preserve, to talk with her further. We fully expected her to talk about attitude, but Lori was full of surprises.

"I give full credit to the comfortable but classic brand of knit pants I first bought in the late 80s, the beret I stumbled across at a garage sale in the mid-90s and the vibrant lipstick that doesn't feather in 2001. About once every five years or so, I stumble across what I call 'a keeper,' and voila, the evolution of what you call my 'style.'"

Lori went on to explain her philosophy of style. "In my view, style is not the result of something you have or don't have. Rather, it is the result of hundreds of good decisions made over a long period of time. Therefore, rather than seeing time as the enemy, it stands to figure that the older you are, the more time you've had to experiment with makeup, clothing, hairstyles and colors and so on and on. In fact, it should hardly be surprising that the more years you've had, the more style you've got."

Tomorrow morning, when you wash your face, put on your makeup and get dressed, celebrate each and every decision you've made that makes your routine possible. Enjoy the feel of the soap and lotion on your face, remember when and where you first purchased the blush and brush, how nice it felt to buy new shoes and how when you found them, you were able to make peace with both comfort and fashion. Think how much you've learned about what it is that makes you feel good and look your best. When you're ready to go, take an extra moment at the mirror and see yourself not just as who you are today—but as the cumulative wisdom of years of experimentation, trial and error and discovery that have allowed you to become more of who you truly are.

54
Beauty and Power

———◦———

As the story goes, the beautiful young woman gets her moment in the spotlight, discovering that her power to turn a head also opens doors for her. But sooner or later, there comes a point where she begins to notice that it is taking more time, products and services to look the same now as she did ten or twenty years ago. No amount of effort can preserve her youthful beauty forever.

Only when her youthful looks transition into something more mature, does she come to realize that what she had valued most all along was not beauty for beauty's sake—but rather, the power that her beauty commanded.

Now she realizes something more. Her youthful beauty was never the only attribute that supplied power, but it was her beauty that was most readily visible to others. She has also been intuitive, creative, educated, diligent and empathetic. And these are but a few of the qualities and characteristics that quietly carried so much of the load, while her beauty got so much of the credit.

While we as well as others may note that our looks are changing, we would be mistaken, indeed, if we miss the fact that our power is still growing as we are able, at last, to acknowledge, cultivate and give proper credit where credit is due.

55

On Being Invisible

———•●•———

J ackie, a striking professor of women's studies in her sixties, spoke for many of the women in our research circles when she named her number one complaint about growing older—"invisibility."

"The thing is, when you feel invisible, you begin to notice that it's harder to get your opinion taken seriously—if it's heard at all. You begin to feel more and more marginalized."

While Jackie spoke this with personal conviction, the truth is that we had seen her in action many times, standing in front of groups of young students, challenging her younger colleagues at coffee hour and in random social situations with people of all ages, and being anything but impotent.

"What's your secret?" we inquired.

"I refuse to incorporate marginalization into my psyche. In fact, I have learned that even if I no longer merit a salacious whistle as I walk past a construction site, I have the capacity to make myself be seen and to be reckoned with when it really matters. Picking my occasions, I'll fight to be heard, if necessary, challenging both the external stereotypes that devalue my potential to make a contribution, and my own temptation to feel sorry for myself, my ego bruised by having lost the biological edge."

Jackie paused, and smiled. "But there's something else, too. I've learned that sometimes, when I so choose, invisibility can be turned to my advantage. After all, it's no accident that along with the ability to bend steel with one's bare hands, invisibility is also a superpower!"

56

The Nature of Desire

Writer Gail Sheehy recalls a trip to Esalen Institute to attend a conference for women 50 and over. It is well known that taking the plunge into the deliciously heated hot tubs at Esalen is something that takes place out in the open air, completely au natural. Gail writes: "I was not expecting to see the more dignified specimens in their late fifties, sixties, and seventies strip down and slip into the famous Esalen hot tubs. But I did. And it was even more startling to note that their bodies were still soft-skinned and feminine in contour. They moved in the water with obvious sensuous pleasure and spontaneity."

For Gail, her visit to the hot tubs at Esalen was a revelation. How could she not have been surprised? When, exactly, do we see the nude bodies of women at midlife and beyond presented as objects of beauty, desire or even intimacy? When, in fact, do we see the sensuous unveiled curves of women in this age group either in person, or portrayed in the movies, in print advertisements or even as art?

The answer is, "Rarely." And yet, how odd this hush, especially when juxtaposed against the pleasure of seeing, naked flesh being warmed in the heated water of open-air hillside tubs.

We are so unused to this that it is with a certain delicacy that we propose, as with beauty in general, that our sexuality is also on a continuum. Some women love their spouses but are content to cuddle and nuzzle or simply enjoy a cup of coffee seated by her beloved's side. But, too, there are women who have found it important and desirable to keep physical passion alive. Some have even found themselves falling in love for the first time, lighting up the night with sizzling affairs. Admittedly, in the absence of conversation, left alone with your desires, you may have assumed a mantle of guilt for any one of a number of reasons. You may be feeling shame for continuing to crave sex. Or you may be feeling equally guilty for preferring to sit close to one another before a blazing fire as opposed to being sexually active.

Reverend Karen Boland, addresses the issue of desire in a tape titled "Woman Awareness." Says Karen: "A true desire is always for a greater expression of ourselves—of life and of love. A true desire is love choosing a direction in which to flow."

This, then, is our common ground: understanding that our desire for intimacy is always good, whatever the form it takes. At last, you can stop wondering if you are normal or deserving, and give yourself permission to bring expression to the deepest behests of your heart in your own, unique way.

57
La Dolce Vita

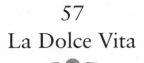

In case of ego emergency, Cynthia—a woman in her fifties who prefers being single but loves attention from attractive men who appreciate a more mature woman—has great advice:

"Pack light, dress tight,
and get your butt on the first plane to Italy."

58

Recognizing Beauty

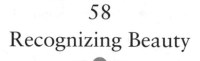

Somewhere, there are women in our generation whose mothers always made them feel beautiful—who lavished compliments, esteem and even awe as they tied pretty ribbons into their daughters' hair. But as for the rest of us, generosity of praise from our mothers tended to be the exception rather than the rule.

The mothers of our generation were cut from a different fabric. As a group, they tended toward strong parenting, administering large doses of reality in order to prepare their daughters for the rigors of life. Many of their offspring were urged not to rely on the beauty card to unlock our destinies, but rather, to develop our other talents and qualities. We listened, and became the most highly educated, most career-oriented generation of women in history. But not to be deterred, we also found a way to redefine beauty for ourselves and for our times, embracing the originality of a Barbara Streisand, the spunk of a Bette Midler, the radiance of an Oprah—whatever size she happened to be at any given time. What most of us lacked in Miss America looks, we made up for with style. Our own special beauty found its way into the world and we blossomed.

And then, life hands us yet another irony. For at the moment when we are called upon to witnesses and care for our own mothers' mortality, we look into the mirror and see changes that unsettle us. In the tumult of life's transitions, the boundaries between our mothers and ourselves may blur, and if we're not careful, we can forget that we are of completely different generations and we still have a long way to go.

And so it was, several years ago, that Amy sat beside her own mother, who had recently moved from her hospital bed to hospice care. Her eyes were dimmed. Rhoda could no longer see her daughter, who at that moment, both felt and looked much older than her years.

Amy had always dreaded her mother's judgments about her looks, calling attention to the weight she had put on, the need for a haircut, and so on and on. Amy judged her mother's looks as well, praying that nobody would ever offer up the misguided compliment "you look just like your Mom."

Now, at long last, the drama was coming to an end. As she sat beside her mother, she forgot all that, feeling only love and gratitude for all the gifts her mother had given her all her life, and forgiving the rest.

Her mother slipping away, they sat quietly together, holding hands. And then, breaking the silence, Amy heard her mother whisper: "How beautiful you look today."

It is the love in our hearts that makes us beautiful and that allows us at last to see the beauty in our mothers as well.

59
Red Dragonfly

Have you ever watched a sunrise, allowing yourself to be uplifted unexpectedly by the in-breaking of beauty? Have you ever found yourself looking up at a clear, starry night, your breath taken away by the immensity of the universe? Have you ever delighted in the unexpected sight of a red dragonfly landing on a lily pad?

Sometimes, there are those moments when you are overcome by the feeling that everything is beautiful—and that you are part of a whole far greater than whatever private judgments you have suffered.

If you want to know the real truth about beauty, tear yourself away from your mirror, with all of its noisy feedback and judgments, and listen, instead, to the wise women among us who have a secret to share. They have figured out that beauty is not about how we look—but rather, beauty is what we crave.

60
The Beauty Ratio

The less time you spend worrying
about what others think of your looks—and the more time
you spend loving yourself—the more beautiful you will be.
Your natural beauty radiates to the exact degree
that your heart has become open and free.

BEAUTY

THE FEAR
*It is a matter of external judgment about whether
you are beautiful or not.*

THE TRUTH
*Beauty is not about how we look—but rather,
beauty is what we crave.*

Health

We know it's important to exercise, to eat right and especially,
    to reduce our anxiety and stress.
Why is it, then, that so often even our best efforts to be healthy
    are driven by fear?

It's no wonder that so many of us approach staying well as a struggle,
    in a world where healthy people are winners and those who
    become sick, losers—
    and ill health a sign of weakness or punishment.

Try, instead, loving your body to its full potential for health, joy and
    vitality,
    knowing that there are times when it is appropriate to do
    everything you can to beat the odds,
    and other times when we must surrender and receive.

Take care of yourself at your deepest levels, and know this:
Whatever life brings your way, you always have the freedom to
    make good choices.
And the most healing choice of all is this: to handle the
    challenges that arise
    not only with a mighty sword,
    but with a mighty heart.

61
The Question of Longevity

——••——

Noneof us really took the Beatle's notion of what it would mean to be 64 seriously, even back when we were adolescents and Paul started singing wryly about getting old. Did Paul McCartney, the eternal youth, really worry about wasting away, about becoming homeless, apathetic, hungry or unloved?

On the other hand, few of us had any idea back then how things would really be for Sir McCartney in his sixties: leaping across stages of sold-out coliseums, raising a toddler and spooning with his new love in embarrassingly public ways.

The fact is that we don't really know what it means to be 64 any more—or 49 or 72 or 87, for that matter. We are living longer and healthier than any generation in history. The average American lifespan has increased by three decades since the early 1900s. And this transpired even before researchers began slowing down the aging process by tinkering with our DNA.

To many of us, scientific, medical and technological advances that raise our odds for increased longevity sound like good news. Statistics hold out the hope of a healthy old age, but most of us have already lived long enough to have had personal brushes with serious illness and loss. Even if we haven't been touched directly, the headline news warns us about a range of threats to our health and security, reminding us hourly that we are mortal. As a generation, we relate to life as if we are going to live forever—but may die tomorrow—all at the same time.

The good news is that many of us have spent many years preparing ourselves to live with uncertainty in ways that generations before us did not. We have had access to spiritual and philosophical traditions from around the world. We have done our personal growth work. We have always been a powerful group of women— powerful socially, economically and spiritually—and we see no reason to stop being powerful now.

So here's the real question about longevity.
Not: What does it mean to be 64, 73 or 92?
But: How would we like it to be?

62

The Body, Mind and Spirit Quiz

Have you ever thought the following?

1. I have a hard time getting the information I need from my physician.
2. I feel guilty that I don't exercise more or that I eat too much of the wrong foods.
3. If something is wrong with a part of my body, I expect that there will be some medication or procedure that will fix it.
4. I am reluctant to question a medical decision.
5. I fear that having a physical problem is a sign of weakness or personal failure.

INTERPRETATION

If you answered yes to any of the above, you have bought into a model of medicine that has taught you to believe that your body is a machine. According to this model of health and healing, it is your responsibility to keep your body running efficiently, and you can do so simply by following the rules.

The problem with the model is this. No woman gets to be our age without realizing that not every problem can be prevented simply by eating more tofu and walking thirty minutes a day—and that not every procedure patches up the broken places good as new. Often, the hierarchy bustles with macho bravado, treating and over-treating your symptoms for as long as the insurance holds out. At worst, it dismisses you as difficult: a loser who has brought misfortune down upon yourself.

Defiantly, the women of our generation who have made peace with their bodies refuse to confuse a failure in the model with a failure in them. Rachel Naomi Remen, M.D., Christiane Northrup, M.D., and Candace Pert, Ph.D. are a few of the visionary doctors and researchers who are working to replace the old medical models that generated fear and shame, with an expanded understanding of our innate capacity to nurture our bodies, minds and spirits for optimum health and healing. We are, in fact, in the early stages of a health revolution that views our relationships to our bodies not as tests of mechanical proficiency—but as initiations into the deeper mysteries of life.

Central to this transformation is the embrace of a more feminine understanding of how bodies heal. "The world 'health' itself is so interesting because it comes from a root that means 'whole'," explains Candace Pert, Ph.D., visiting professor at the Center for Molecular and Behavioral Neuroscience, Rutgers University. Dr. Pert discovered peptide receptors in the brain and body, which demonstrated scientifically what mystics have known for millennia: there is a tangible connection among body, mind and spirit.

"The mind is some kind of enlivening energy in the information realm throughout the brain and body that enables the cells to talk to each other, and the outside to talk to the whole organism... Part of being a healthy person is being well integrated and at peace, with all of the systems acting together."

In her book *Woman As Healer*, Dr. Jeanne Achterberg describes this holistic consciousness as having been "born out of crisis and frustration with living in a rather constant state of disease... The healing consciousness that embodies the feminine recognizes that we are all part of a living, breathing, global entity. The focus on the health of human tissue alone—without similar due concern for feelings, spirituality, relationships, and the environment upon which all health, all life is dependent, is dangerously myopic."

Of course, when we set the goal of optimizing our potential for health or healing, we want the scientific facts, the medical research, the latest technology—not to mention the inspirational stories of women who beat the odds. And we want something more. We want our integrity: a quality of life, regardless of our diagnoses, that reflects our deepest values. It is this new model, in fact, that creates the environment in which our optimal health is most likely to transpire.

63

On Having a Senior Moment

———●———

Miriam is known for her witty quips and off-the-cuff humor, but she did not laugh when upon momentarily forgetting her production assistant's name, the producer who was eavesdropping kidded her about having "a senior moment."

Miriam responded: "If a young person momentarily loses a word, you don't call it a 'junior moment,' do you? But if you're a mature woman, and you can't remember a name, suddenly you're suspected of losing your faculties."

The producer was taken aback by Miriam's anger, more concerned about Miriam losing her sense of humor than her mind. But Miriam persisted.

A director of documentaries who had won numerous awards, Miriam explained that what bothered her most is that so many of her generation think of "having a senior moment" as an innocuous, even charming, self-effacement when, in truth, the phrase is indicative of an onerous stereotype of aging.

"When you refer to yourself as having a 'senior moment,' it is as if you are saying to the world that you should be held to a lesser standard: that in one of the most critical areas of all—your brain function—you are no longer fully accountable. You have, in fact, allowed yourself to become a victim of outdated biases about aging, feeding directly into other people's prejudices."

And the prejudices add up. How many times does a woman of our generation have legitimate symptoms to report to her physician, only to be dismissed by the doctor as suffering from nothing more than "old age." Ironically, physicians often lump many of these symptoms—such as dizziness, fuzziness, exhaustion—into this category, dismissing them as normal, if unfortunate, signs of aging, when, in actuality, they are often easily correctable side-effects of drugs prescribed for other conditions.

But here's an equally chilling notion to consider when it comes to senior moments and the like: how many times can you joke about infirmity before you, yourself, start believing it to be true?

64
Consult Your Body

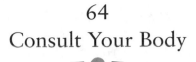

Rosalind is a well-known artist who woke up one day with her shoulder frozen in pain. It was the last thing she needed, under the gun as she was to complete a commission that was already overdue. Her physician ordered surgery, promising that she would have immediate relief. When she awoke in the hospital, her shoulder was throbbing and even after several weeks, the pain persisted. A second and then a third operation quickly followed.

With little improvement, she found herself once again draped in a flimsy hospital gown, lying still in the cold metal belly of the high-tech MRI tunnel, an intimidating machine, scanning her body for clues. It was then, feeling exposed and vulnerable, that Rosalind overheard two technicians talking about her body as if she were an object consisting solely of tendons, muscles and adhesions. As Rosalind tells it: "It wasn't more than a few months ago that I thought of myself as a force with whom other people had to contend. In my world, I was one of those people who made things happen. Now, I was patient number 572959: a raggedy-edged rotator cuff with a body attached."

At that moment, she realized that whatever the MRI would uncover could not even come close to capturing the most important parts of herself. She would continue to receive the medical reports and her physician's recommendations as information, but begin participating in her own healing in conscious ways. She would ask more questions, share more of what she was feeling and supplement the medical protocols with approaches that came from listening to her own body, mind and spirit, as well.

As soon as she returned home, she wrote her pain a letter.

"Dear shoulder, please let me know what you need from me to heal."

The symptom responded.

"Dear Rosalind, I've never been your shoulder—I'm your heart. See here, where it really hurts? It's between your shoulder blades in the back, where the back of your heart is. I've been holding my breath ever since you missed the deadline for your commission. That's what's really been frozen. Imagine me breathing and your symptoms will ease up."

Rosalind took her heart's advice. Every time she felt the symptom, she imagined her heart breathing. While her shoulder still ached when she was tired, it was no longer a debilitating problem. She simply visualized her heart breathing and found herself able to paint again. Whatever the cause of her recovery, her physician was both pleased and relieved and Rosalind wryly reports, promptly took all the credit.

Says Dr. Christiane Northrup, who recommends that her patients converse with their ailing body parts whenever advice is needed: "We have inner guidance and spiritual help available that can help us move toward optimal health, joy, and fulfillment... Be eager to listen and slow to judge."

65

Exercise Your Spirit

—■—●—■—

Lisa, the owner of a popular restaurant, arrived at one of our research circles exhausted and stressed out.

"What's happening?" we inquired.

"Yesterday, my doctor told me that he didn't like some of my test readings and that I needed to make a concerted effort to find something to relax me. So I took up knitting."

Lisa had gone straight to the best knitting shop in town, bought enough yarn to knit holiday presents for her whole list and a "teach yourself to knit book." She stayed up most of the night, unable to tear herself away from her needles before compulsively finishing an eight-foot long scarf.

We sympathized with Lisa, having similarly understood "giving it all you've got" to mean "to the limits of human endurance, and then some." If it doesn't feel punishing, on some level, we wonder how effective it could possibly be.

But often, particularly for the high-achieving women of our generation, when it comes to staying or getting healthy, the solution is doing less, not more. This is not something many of us are naturally good at, so here is a suggestion to get you started.

Find a leafy green tree and sit beneath it for half an hour, your back resting comfortably against the bark of the trunk. Make sure you do this before noon, while the tree is taking rejuvenating strength out of the earth through its roots and carrying it upwards to its light-seeking branches. Let yourself receive effortlessly, feeling the tree's regenerative energy bringing you new sources of strength.

66
Why Did I Create This?

———● ●●———

Whe Jenny's best friend was diagnosed with a serious illness, she became obsessed with taking better care of her own health. Already exercising regularly and watching her diet, she decided to pick up the pace, scanning the web for hours at a time, searching for the latest preventative theories. Understanding the connection between body, mind and spirit, she decided to add a hypnotherapist to her growing regime of therapies. After hearing everything she was doing for herself, the hypnotherapist smiled.

"Ah, you're in the magic bullet stage," she offered.

"What's that?"

"That desperate moment when you think if only you could get it exactly right, you could be in complete control of your destiny."

This would be a logical conclusion, considering how many self-help books, pop psychologists and positive-thinking practices center on the same message: You can learn to call the shots in your life. You just have to work hard enough at it, be positive enough, good enough, spiritual enough, and you can get what you want. We can't help but applaud the indomitability of the human spirit. But there's a price for the applause. For the underlying message is this: if you do have it within your means to control your destiny through your will, then if you do become ill, you must have been responsible for that, as well.

"Why did you create your illness?" is a question that lies deep in one's unconscious. It is also a question that, unfortunately, is likely to be posed to you by supportive family and friends, bosses and even a well-meaning stranger who gently suggests that those who become ill are somehow at fault.

The fact that so many of us are willing to ask and answer the question, "Why did I create this?" is an indication of how terrified we are of losing control. Jenny's hypnotherapist suggested that they use their time together not to plumb her unconscious looking for buried death wishes and fatal flaws, but to provide an opportunity for her to reconnect with her faith.

"You see, Jenny, you think it's all up to you. The truth is that to refuse to take on the responsibility for creating illness is to admit with deepest humility that you are human and so you are, by definition, limited. None of us will get through life without butting up against issues. But the irony is this: you create the best possible environment for optimizing your potential for health by motivating yourself out of life and acceptance, rather than fear."

67
One More Lesson

———•———

We asked Lucy, one of the wisest women we know, the secret of a long life.

"Eighteen years ago, I got a tumor on my spine," she replied.

"The doctor told me I needed surgery. But I refused his recommendation. Instead, for ten years, I followed every alternative therapy I could get my hands on. I used herbs, I meditated, I went to an acupuncturist and a great therapist. I got amazing insights from my healing process. Because of the tumor, my life went through an inspiring transformation."

"And then it cleared up?"

"No. For ten years, I got every kind of mental, physical, and spiritual lesson you could possibly get from a tumor, and still it didn't go away.

"Finally, I said 'Oh hell,' and got the damn thing out."

68
Initiation

Stories about the victory of the human spirit over cancer are inspiring. But common sense—and the holistic approach to body-mind-spirit that many of us have been following since the 60s—would suggest that when your body is ill, you need to nurture yourself: not go into battle. Of course, we all need balance in our lives: times when we are driving ourselves through force of will, and times when we are taking care of ourselves at the deepest levels. This is true for all of us, and doubly true for people dealing with serious illnesses, such as cancer. Cancer cells are part of our bodies that don't recognize their own limitations, after all.

Ironically, the cancer culture honors exactly those traits that may contribute to our own immune system's exhaustion: raging, racing, and fighting to win. As members of the "make love not war" generation, many of us are reluctant to wage a war that includes raising the sword against parts of our bodies—even parts that have gone awry. Surely there is some other metaphor that could be both inspirational and life giving.

So it was for four women who underwent successful treatment for breast cancer around the same time a number of years ago. None identified with the warfare terminology and together, they set out to develop a new language for speaking about breast cancer and other serious illnesses.

They began thinking of breast cancer as initiation, not battle, recognizing that allowing themselves to be vulnerable would be a better way to be in the world. They came to understand that true power is not only knowing when to push—to struggle against the odds—but also, when to let go. Sometimes, you even have to relax and allow yourself be a sick person who relies on other people and sources of strength.

The four women introduced their language for healing in the book they wrote together: *Speak the Language of Healing*. Here is an adapted excerpt:

HOW TO SPEAK THE LANGUAGE OF HEALING

Instead of saying	Say
I am a victim of cancer	I was diagnosed with cancer on...
I am fighting cancer	I am in treatment for breast cancer
She lost her battle with cancer	Cancer was the cause of her death
The War on Cancer	Advances in cancer research and treatment
I survived (or beat) cancer	I'm healthy

Whatever the health challenges you may face, know this: it's not just about winning the battle. It's about choosing to live whatever life one has been blessed with to the fullest. This is our only real responsibility. Not "How will I beat this disease?" but "Am I willing to be transformed by whatever life brings my way?"

69
Along with Flowers...

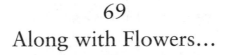

It's a fact. Most people are uncomfortable around illness. Even when meaning to show support, people will often say or do things that are likely to make a challenging time even more difficult. Here are some conversation guidelines you might like to share with others, preferably before the need arises.

CONVERSATION GUIDELINES FOR VISITORS

1. Please don't ask me "how are you?" How I may be feeling is lousy. Instead, just let me know that you're happy to see me. If you are leaving me a phone message, simply let me know that you are sending good thoughts my way.

2. Please don't give me unsolicited medical advice. You may be burning to share your theory about which doctor, hospital or treatment I should really be utilizing, but before you blurt it out, ask for my permission. For instance, you can inquire—in a non-leading way—"Are you happy with your hospital?" If I am, then button it up. If not, feel free to ask, "Would you like me to do some research on other possibilities, or offer you some suggestions?"

3. Please don't use me as your sounding board. I am a captive audience and it would be gracious of you not to succumb to the temptation to use me for therapy. It would, in fact, help if you came equipped with something upbeat or interesting to talk about. And, if that's not what I need, give me the space to vent, angst or cry without thinking you can or should do anything about it. Remember that you are coming to give, not get. And one of the greatest contributions to my healing that you can make is unconditional love and a time-out from judgment.

4. Please don't refer to my illness as a gift. Yes, we can learn from the things that happen to us—even illness. But did I really need this great gift or lesson more than you or anybody else? As a wise woman once commented: "If this ailment is such a gift, do you know anybody who takes returns?"

70
What a Ride

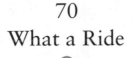

Of course, it is important to do what you can to stay
healthy. But just as important is how you go about doing
it. We all know women who are obsessed with staying
healthy, doing everything in their power to keep aging at bay. Some
attempt to beat their bodies into submission, some cringe in an
effort to self-protect.

What's the alternative?

To live your life fully, you create your best chances for optimal
health by motivating yourself out of love, not fear. Love having fun,
love taking care of yourself and others, love doing foolish and self-
indulgent things, love taking risks, falling short, dusting yourself off
and trying again.

An anonymous message that arrived recently via email captures
this sentiment eloquently.

"Life should not be a journey to the grave with the intention of
arriving safely in an attractive and well preserved body, but rather
to skid in sideways, chocolate in hand, your body thoroughly used
up, totally worn out and screaming—WOO HOO what a ride!"

HEALTH

THE FEAR
*Having less than perfect health
is a sign of weakness or punishment.*

THE TRUTH
*Loving yourself, no matter what, creates the environment
in which your optimal health is most likely to transpire.*

Inevitabilities:
Caregiving, Loss
and Mortality

Standing as reluctant witnesses at the threshold of mortality,
more is often asked of us than we think we have to give.
And sadly, many of us come to discover that not every ending is a
happy one.
If you are not careful, you may mistake this unveiling of the
illusions as your own personal failure,
Or be tempted to rage against life and others who have let you
down.
Instead, you must do the impossibly brave: facing loss and
inevitability head-on,
remembering that your appointed task is not to save,
but to love...
and braver still, to forgive not only yourself,
but the human condition.

71

Caregiving and Caretaking

———◆———

Here is what social analysts are telling us.

- Given unprecedented longevity, not only of our own generation but of our parents' generation as well, the average American woman can expect to spend more years caring for her parents than she did caring for her children.
- Ninety percent of unpaid caregivers providing assistance to the disabled elderly at home are women.
- Twenty-two percent of family caregivers quit paying jobs in order to spend more than 18 hours a day serving as home nurses for no pay.

Nothing about this is fair. Even though, or perhaps especially when, we deeply love those for whom we care, it's not fair to have so much of the work of caretaking fall on our already-burdened shoulders. And that's just the beginning of the injustices, for from where we stand, becoming disabled isn't fair, either. Neither is sickness nor, while we're at it, is death. Not everything is a blessing, even in disguise. Things are not always deserved. What happens to us or others does not always make sense.

This is not to say that we cannot strive to be the kind of people who grow in profound ways through everything that life brings our way, fair or not. And what life is bringing to many of our generation right now is the need to witness and appropriately attend not only an extended period of longevity, but of dying.

The implications are many and profound. For one thing, it means that the stages of mourning that once fell upon us like an avalanche at the end of a loved one's life—numbness, anger, negotiation, grief, acceptance—now unravel slowly like a dense, tangled ball of yarn over an extended period of time. The emotions double-up on themselves, wrapping around each other like resistant knots, tangling and untangling when you least expect it. Some of us may not even have our own adult children out of the house before the first of our parents requires extra help. If you are married to someone older than you, you may be handling two generations at once. And sometimes, sadly, it is our adult children, themselves, who need our assistance. Three generations are spinning around us like plates on sticks.

Even if you are fortunate enough to count your inner circle's good health among today's blessings, you still cannot avoid the daily body count of tragedies due to terrorism, natural disaster and violent crime streaming in to you from around the world. We are all having to learn a new skill that we wish we could have been lucky, smart, rich and powerful enough to have developed on our own: how to co-exist with mortality.

"We are always dying a bit, always giving things up, always having things taken away... There are no turning points that are not accompanied by feelings of dying," offers psychotherapist Stanley Keleman, referring to the transition points in our lives as "daily little deaths."

We die a little death when our children go off to school for the first time, and another little death when they graduate to start their own lives. We die a little death every time we lose a job, a friend, a dream. We die a little death the first time we need glasses to read, or when we can't quite make out what someone is saying to us in a crowded room.

When someone for whom we care becomes ill, the little deaths pile up on one another. A disability, the diminishment of the senses, hours of pain that were once precious moments for productivity, conversation and the possibility for mutual joy: for us, the caregivers, the lesson of coexisting with mortality becomes obvious early on. We who have answered life's cry take up the sacred task of tending love's flame through the dark night. We dig deep to find the words we've previously neglected to say, feel things we hadn't realized were there before, all the while confronting the humbling reality that we know less than ever before. Just when everything seems so very important, we are at our most helpless, searching for the best thing to say or do, trying to get it right.

At the very moment we need our greatest strength, we are our most vulnerable. And yet, somehow, we find it in ourselves to give more than we thought we had in us. We bear more pain than we ever thought possible. And we become greedy for whatever joy and hope life offers up along the way.

In doing so, we find ourselves able to turn even darkness into sacred space.

72
The Sesame Seed

———• ● •———

There is a famous story from the Buddhist tradition that is helpful to remember when you or someone you love is suffering. As the story goes, a woman who is grieving goes to the Buddha and asks him to lift the burden of her sorrows and restore her lost loved one to her. Buddha listens compassionately, then gives the woman a mysterious instruction.

′ "Go to the village and knock on doors, asking to receive but a single sesame seed from any home that has not suffered a loss such as yours."

The woman set out and began knocking on doors, but nowhere did she find a house that did not know grief. Empty-handed, she returned to the Buddha and understanding the nature of the learning, became enlightened.

Nothing feels more personal than suffering, but in truth, there is nothing more universal. Buddha could not restore the woman's loss, but he could restore her peace of mind.

THE SESAME SEED

There was a time when you thought you were calling the shots
   in your life:
Work hard, Be good, Be smart, and things would turn out for you.
There was a time when you thought you knew things,
When you protected yourself and others from the hard places.
You felt big and strong and capable.
In sacred space, things spin out of control.
Our tender vulnerabilities stand exposed.
But in the emptiness that we once filled mostly with ourselves
There is now, at last, a space big enough for God.

73

The Ecology of Living

One is not liable for what one says while suffering.
THE TALMUD

Even though most of us grew up and left our families of origin many years ago, the decline of a parent can throw us back into childhood patterns quickly. Which role were you assigned to play in your family? Were you the good girl, the dependable one? Or were you the bad girl, in perennial need of redemption? However hard you've worked at putting some degree of separation between you and the rivalries, negotiations and alliances of your family's past, confrontation with mortality snaps everything into reverse.

All at once, you are meant to be in some kind of teamwork with people who may not always remember that forty years have passed since you lived under the same roof. You may have moved to the other side of the world, established your own career, raised your own children, and yet here you are, dealing with the temper tantrums of a two-year-old, the maneuvering of a ten-year-old, the rebellion of a 13-year old. Only these aren't your children or grandchildren. These are your adult brothers and sisters, your extended family, your parents and yes, even your own upset self. Emotional pasts often take on lives of their own.

At our best, we are all able to adapt to changing times, needs and circumstances, discovering our profound capacity to establish what Joan Erikson refers to so eloquently as "the ecology of living."

In the context of ecology, caregiving calls upon us to move beyond the individuation and separation we worked so hard to establish in early adulthood, and put our trust in interdependence. "Human beings need one another, and their vital involvement in relationships nourishes and sustains the whole cycle of life. This is the law of the natural world. The acceptance of it as a fundamental precept can dispose us to find our places, as it were, organically on this planet," writes Joan.

In the healthy ecology, no one has to be the one who is strong all the time. The declining parent who has always been so eager to give, must now learn to receive. The primary caretaker upon whom all others depend can learn to ask for help. We do not find ourselves frozen in old roles and patterns, but open ourselves, even if painfully, to new relationships and facets of ourselves, exposed not despite but because of our growing mutuality.

This is the best-case scenario. But sadly, the people upon whom we wish we could depend do not always rise to the occasion. In many families, we never do quite pull it together, bumping along side-by-side—and sometimes into one another—navigating the uncharted waters of life and death decisions in the dark of night, using old, outdated maps.

The thing is, it's not really a question of whether we love one another. We suffer specifically because we do care so passionately, trying to work out the meaning of our lives in and through each other. We do so, sometimes stupidly, sometimes with unexpected grace and beauty.

The real issue is not can we love, but can we forgive, not only others, but ourselves. And, too, can we forgive the human condition. For sometimes, life really does ask more of us than anyone should ever have to give.

74

Healing Eve

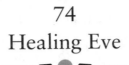

It is a great challenge not to get swept up in other people's agendas for how our lives ought to look. It is sometimes an even greater challenge not to get swept up in other people's ideas about how death is going to be.

Jimmy can still vividly remember a balmy spring day in Texas when she was 12 years old. She was inside her house practicing piano. Her father was working in the garden in the back yard. Having been raised with a hellfire and brimstone version of religion, Jimmy remembers this as one of those rare, happy moments when the entire family was relaxing at home together, rather than at church. Jimmy's brother was in his bedroom coloring. Mother was studying her Bible.

Rapt in the song she was playing, she didn't pay any attention when Mother went outside to call Jimmy's father in for lunch. The next thing she heard was Mother's high-pitched scream. Jimmy rushed outside and found her mother frozen in horror.

"Mother! What's wrong!" she cried out.

Her mother could bare reply.

"It's your father. He's gone!"

"Gone?"

Jimmy's mind raced over the horrible possibilities, bracing herself for tragedy. But before she could contemplate any specifics, mother continued:

"The Rapture has happened and your father has been taken up to the clouds, but I have been left behind!"

Just then, Jimmy's father came around the corner of the house, where he'd been pruning gardenias. Her mother threw herself into his arms, as relieved that she had not missed the rapture as Jimmy was that her father was still alive.

In retrospect, this story may sound amusing. But in the fundamentalist family's reality, hell, the second coming, rapture, were all taken dead seriously. Jimmy was raised to view life as a long prelude to the real pay-off: what happens to us after we die. This message was constantly reinforced, the emphasis placed less on the heaven part, and more on the horrors of burning in the eternal bonfires of hell for any one of a growing list of transgressions. Everything from wearing shorts and going dancing, to secret doubts and fears tucked away into the inner regions of one's frightened heart could draw down upon you the wrath of the vengeful God— so ready and willing to pass harsh judgment.

There are many of our generation who were raised to believe that because of what Eve did in the Garden of Eden, we are wicked and cursed. The scars go deep and while recovery is possible, it is often hard-won, indeed.

Over the past five decades, Jimmy worked hard to move beyond a fear-driven relationship to life. She has, in fact, turned her parents' messages about life and death upside down. Rather than living with fear of the "rapture," Jimmy sees every one of her days as an opportunity to love the world, herself and others as fully as humanly possible.

Jimmy had fought her way back to spiritual and psychological health many years before the first of her parents became ill. By then, she had forgiven them both, reasoning that she had not been privy to their reasons for their religious decisions. No longer living under their roof, and growing a family of her own, she found it possible to be both generous and self-protective.

Then came the ten years—an entire decade—during which she was called upon to tend to the declines and ultimately the deaths of both parents. Even though she lived many states away, the frequency of contact quickly accelerated first to once a month, then to once a week and ultimately, day to day. She was there when her father passed out while touring the cruise captain's cockpit on what turned out to be his last trip. And she was there, her arm around her mother's shoulder, as her mother tried to reckon with her fears of being left behind again, this time for real. She was there when her mother went through a series of painful operations and at both her parents' funerals, not only mourning her losses, but making sure that their final wishes were carried out, as promised.

She faced a seemingly endless stream of hospital chaplains, ministers and missionaries sent to safeguard her parents' souls. Her biggest challenge was how to honor her parents and their beliefs while not compromising her own convictions.

During their extended illnesses, Jimmy could not bring herself to talk to her parents in their terms of heaven and hell, although she was willing to listen quietly, and to embrace and accept that her parents' reality was true for them, even if no longer true for her. Jimmy struggled to do the right things and to find just the right words. Finally, in her father's final days, she found them.

She vividly remembers the feel of her father's frail hand in hers.

"Daddy," Jimmy said at last. "I know where you're going."

He smiled weakly at her. "I do, too."

"Well then," she said, smiling back through her tears, "I'll see you there."

75
Nothing Left Unsaid

A silent prayer for the bedside of someone for whom you care:

I sit here,
Immersed in thoughts and feelings about you.
The ordinary stops and the world recedes.
This is sacred space
Where everyday matters cannot penetrate.
Time stretches out and embraces us.

No need for words.
The depth of suffering is the only bridge to acceptance
and forgiveness that we require.
Drinking deeply of every feeling as if for the first time,
and then breathing together quietly,
our hearts so full, they are breaking.

76
Rules for a Life on Hold

———■●■———

For some people, taking care of a loved one is an extended moment that transcends time and space. It is as if the two of you—and sometimes an expanded circle of friends and family—are sharing one heart. It is possible to sit together, immersed in thoughts and feelings, embraced by sacred space. Even under the most challenging circumstances, it is possible to feel yourself able to rise to many occasions, your spirit growing as ordinary life diminishes. However, it is also possible that despite the love, you will become exhausted. Your ordinary work and life schedules may have to bend in order to accommodate not only your own, but all the emotions and logistics of your loved one's life. You will find yourself engaged in a new, complex world of familial, medical and professional relationships, asked to make critical decisions about subjects you know nothing about.

For those who are feeling older, weaker and more vulnerable than they thought they would ever have to feel at their age, here are some guidelines we've gathered from the library of communal wisdom to which so many of us have already contributed, to help you through this most difficult of times.

1. Don't make any more decisions about your own life than you absolutely have to at this juncture. You've got your hands full taking care of another.
2. The kinds of decisions we're talking about here are not only about career moves, selling homes and the like, but also about the meaning of life.
3. When it all becomes too much for you, ask for help and take a break.
4. Remember that you are not the one who is dying. You have your own destiny and it is critical that you not leap to assumptions about how your future will be.

77

The Mortal Wound

The maxim of illusory religion runs: "Fear not,
trust in God and He will see that none of the things you fear
will happen to you." That of real religion, on the contrary, is
"Fear not: The things that you are afraid of are quite likely
to happen to you, but they are nothing to be afraid of."
J. MACMURRAY, _Persons in Relation_

There are times in our lives when our hearts are filled with sorrow, not celebration. There are times when we feel anxiety, doubt, and fear instead of certainty. When we suffer through these darkest hours, experiencing what Thomas Moore in _Care of the Soul_ calls "the mortal wound," we find ourselves feeling ashamed of ourselves, believing that going through this should be less difficult than it is.

At these times, those who have traveled this most difficult stretch of life's journey guide us to turn towards rather than away from the pain. Melodie Beattie, who lost her son in a tragic skiing accident, advises:

"Surrender to the moment. Ride it out and through, for all it's worth. Throw yourself into it. Stop resisting. So much of the anguish is created when we are in resistance. So much relief, release, and change are possible when we accept, simply accept. We waste our time, expend our energy, and make things harder by resisting, repressing, and denying."

When you give up resistance, allowing your losses to loosen your grip on the illusion of control, you leave behind ordinary definitions of success and failure. In depths you had not previously known, you begin to sense that you are in a process. Life is waiting patiently for you to remember its embrace. But beware! For the cost of returning to life is great. There will be times when you will feel that you have been directed to march off the edge of a cliff, with only the endless void of the infinite to break your fall. Will it? If you are always sure that everything will go back to the way things were, you are still clinging to the edge. The order you envision is quite simply not the order of the divine. Your only real hope is to rise and fall on the ever-changing tides of dread and awe. When you become certain, you fall. When you are cast out, you are found. Only when you become willing to embrace the whole range of human experience, death as well as life, do you remove the impediments that separate you from connection to the divine mystery.

This, then, is sacred space, the realm of the true mystic: not the illusion of tamed order, delivering outcomes on demand as a reward for your obedience. But rather, creation out of chaos, the terror of plummeting through deep mystery, wrestling with your own embarrassing finitude. And then, impossibly, there are those rare, sublime moments when you experience the divine. As mystic philosopher Charles Kingsley writes:

"When I walk the fields, I am impressed now and then with an innate feeling that everything I see has a meaning, if I could but understand it. And this feeling of being surrounded with truths which I cannot grasp amounts to indescribable awe..."

In these moments, you have a sense that you are part of a whole, far greater than whatever losses you have suffered. The diminishment of personal tragedy before the urge for unity with the universe is not a means to an end, but the end itself. Once you have tasted such an awareness, even if but for a moment, you can begin to trust that there is meaning in existence that transcends all. For the spiritually gifted, it becomes more and more possible to set aside your ordinary concerns, to pay attention to the forces greater than but including yourself and those for whom you care, that are luring you forward. The truth is that you do not always know where you are heading, but you can become content being in free fall within the heart of the divine.

78
The Wheel of Life

— ● —

Many of us recognize the work of the late Elisabeth Kubler-Ross, M.D. whose book, *On Death and Dying*, threw her into the center of both medical and theological controversy. In her autobiography, Elisabeth explains that according to her parents, she was supposed to have been "a nice, church-going Swiss housewife." Instead, she ended up "an opinionated psychiatrist, author and lecturer in the American Southwest, who communicates with spirits from a world that I believe is far more loving and glorious than our own."

In the book, Elisabeth tells about her mother's prolonged illness and death. Elisabeth had taken her two children to visit her mother and grandmother in Switzerland. Together, they went on long hikes and spoke of heartfelt matters. At one point, her mother turned to Elisabeth and said "We don't live forever," continuing on that if she ever became a vegetable, she wanted Elisabeth's assurances that she would end her life. Three days later, her mother suffered a massive stroke and remained in a vegetative state for four years. Elisabeth, who saw in death only love and glory, could not bring herself to end her mother's life before God was ready to take her.

"For some reason, God saw fit to keep her alive like this for four more years. I wanted to know why my mother ended up like this. I constantly asked myself what lesson God was trying to teach this loving woman."

For six months, Elisabeth stayed up, writing well into the night, what was to become her third book: *Death: the Final Stage of Growth*.

"From the title alone, you would have thought I had all the answers about death. But on the day I finished, my mother died in the Swiss nursing home where she had spent the past four years, and I found myself asking God why He made this woman who, for eighty-four years, gave only love, shelter and affection, a vegetable and kept her in this state for so long."

Even at her mother's funeral, Elisabeth cursed God for his unkindness.

"Then, as unbelievable as it sounds, I changed my mind."

Spontaneously, Elisabeth found herself thanking God for his generosity. For suddenly, it occurred to her that her mother had one final lesson she had to learn before passing.

"It dawned on me that my mother's final lesson had been to learn how to receive affection and care, something she had never been good at. From then on, I praised God for teaching her in just four years. I mean, it could have been a lot longer."

Elisabeth concludes: "When we have passed the tests we were sent to Earth to learn, we are allowed to graduate. We are allowed to shed our body, which imprisons our soul the way a cocoon encloses the future butterfly, and when the time is right we can let go of it. Then we will be free of pain, free of fears and free of worries...free as a beautiful butterfly returning home to God."

79
Two Pockets

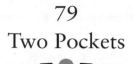

A great spiritual teacher once said to his disciples, "Everyone must have two pockets, so that he can reach into the one or the other, according to his needs." In his left pocket are to be the words: "I am earth and ashes." In his right: "For my sake was the world created."

Here is a special meditation for those of you who find yourself in the presence of one who is dying.

Imagine yourself surrounded by a sphere of light. The sphere of light allows love and forgiveness to pass in and out, but nothing else. Death and dying are repelled by the light and cannot get through to you.

Remember, it is the one for whom you are caring who is dying. You are still alive.

80
The Most Compelling Question

When you have really been through it,
   pummeled and raked,
   punctured and broken
And yet, you show up,
   still game
   ready to struggle for meaning
Only then will you discover that the most compelling question is not:
   "How will one die?" but rather
   "How will one live?"

INEVITABILITIES:

CAREGIVING, LOSS AND MORTALITY

THE FEAR
In your struggles with decline, loss and mortality—
you are doomed to fail.

THE TRUTH
Decline, loss and mortality is a natural part of the life cycle,
something with which you have no choice but to make peace.

Creating a Legacy

Awash in a world of needs and opportunities,
    we strive to leave our mark on generations to come:
    to know that we were here and that our lives mattered.

Of course, we should do what we can,
    sharing our wisdom, energy and resources with others
    and contributing however and whatever we can
    to make a difference.

But remember that our everyday lives provide us with many
    occasions for greatness,
    not only when we are doing things of great significance,
    but also when we approach whatever's next with great love.

81

The Greatest Treasure

————— ● —————

Through all the world there goes one long cry from the heart...
"Give me leave to do my utmost."
ISAK DINESEN, *Babette's Feast*

"Are you reading anything interesting?" Allen O'Brien asked Jimmy, when they were introduced to one another at a social gathering some years ago. Jimmy loves to read, so it was no surprise that she had a ready reply. At the time, Jimmy was in the middle of Irving Stone's *The Greek Treasure*, the story of Heinrich Schliemann who in the late 1800s used his own money to excavate the mythical city of Troy.

"Really!" Allen O'Brien responded. "Have you thought about studying archeology? I'd be glad to introduce you to some brilliant archeologists and paleoanthropologists, and tell you about some exciting digs you might want to join."

Jimmy's heart leapt at the thought, but the notion of actually becoming an archeologist, traveling the world in search of the earth's hidden secrets, seemed to her at the time to be an impossible dream. She explained to Allen that she had her hands full, being a wife, mother and real estate broker.

"So what?" Allen said. "When I was forty, I left my career as an entrepreneur to set out to map unknown rivers." In fact, Allen had become an adventurer, traveling to Africa, India and many corners of the world.

Inspired by Allen's words, Jimmy decided that at the very least, she could take one course in archeology at the local college. One course led to another and over ten years, to the completion of her undergraduate, masters and then doctoral degrees. Along the way, she visited archeological digs around the world. In Tanzania, she walked the site where archeologists had discovered hominid skulls over 1.75 million years old. In Johannesburg, Jimmy held the skeleton of the famous Taung child, over two million years old.

The last time she saw Allen, they both had many destinations on their wish lists. But shortly thereafter, the phone rang. A mutual friend was on the line, telling Jimmy that Allen had chartered a small airplane in search of a small bird sanctuary on a tiny island off the coast of India. The weather was inclement and the plane had gone down, killing all on board. Jimmy was devastated at the loss.

Not long after, Jimmy received another call. This one was from one of the "brilliant paleonanthropologists" to whom she'd been introduced by Allen. The director of the Institute of Human Origins, Donald Johanson, discoverer of the 3.75 million-year-old hominid, Lucy, was on the line. "Would you consider becoming a board member?" Jimmy looked up to the heavens and said to Allen, "So this is what you had in mind for me!"

Through friendship and example, Allen showed Jimmy the importance of paying heed to the divine spark that we have within us, holding the potential to connect each of us to something greater than ourselves. For Allen, the pursuit of his dreams wasn't about doing something significant, important or even noticeable—it was about living his life to the fullest.

Jimmy realized that through her friendship with Allen, she had unearthed her greatest treasure. It wasn't the hidden city of Troy, nor was it any of the artifacts or hidden rivers already crossed off either of their lists. Rather, it was the heart of the seeker's own self , entreating one to defy both reason and doubt to embark upon the adventure of one's life.

82

On Generosity

———•———

One rainy day, Marcy's mother called her from her retirement center to say that she urgently needed Marcy to come take her to the grocery store. Over ninety, Sarah was rapidly going blind and needed the assistance of a walker to get around. Marcy did not hesitate. It sounded important, indeed.

When they got to the store, before getting out of the car, Sarah looked around disappointedly and said: "We need to go to another store."

"Why?" Marcy inquired.

"Because the homeless woman who is usually here must be somewhere else. I need to find her to give her my umbrella."

Some see charity and good works as duty. Others see it as an act of love. While either can be beneficial, the latter multiplies the effects of goodness exponentially.

Money Magazine, in a December '04 article on "Charitable Giving" suggests that "the closer the match between your giving and your passions, the greater the reward you will feel." To accomplish this, the article suggests four steps to consider taking before selecting your charitable involvement.

1. "Find Your Motivation." Don't just do what 60% of households do, which is respond to a solicitation. Instead, be proactive in identifying the causes that matter most to you, taking a leading role in making your philanthropic contributions.

2. "Check Out the Charity." Gather the information you need regarding how the charities that address your concern or issue make use of their funds to support their mission. "If a charity's numbers seem troubling and you have no easy way to check the situation further, move on."

3. "Consider the Impact." How urgently does the organization truly need the money? There are a number of worthwhile causes, many close to home, that don't have the big fund raising budgets but do important work in our communities. Give to them and you will be able to keep closer tabs on where the money is going and whether or not it is being utilized effectively.

4. "Leverage Your Giving." Start or join in on a matching grant program or donor-advised fund, a stocks and bonds investment fund that allows a portion of your money to be donated to the charities of your choice.

83
What Matters Most

The world is so big and the needs are so many. How can you sort through all the possibilities to determine what matters most to you?

Begin by writing down every issue or concern that occurs to you over the period of a week. "Do it quickly. Don't let the filters drop into place," says author Jennifer James.

Someone you love has suffered an illness and you wish you could do something to alleviate her suffering. Write it down. You hear that your grandson's school has just had to cut back on its music program, and you think "what a shame." Write it down. Every headline that touches you. Every comment made in passing, to which you feel a twinge, a moan or a sob. Write it down.

At the end of the week, revisit the list and now do the most important thing: cross off everything you think you should or ought to do. "Cross off what your mother wants, what your father wants, what your spouse wants, what your neighbor wants, what other people or your professors want, so that the only thing you have left is what you want. Once you know what it is, then you can make plans to get it," says Jennifer.

84
Dangerous Women

———◂●▸———

In the secret recesses of your heart, there is something that you know is yours to do. Perhaps you have allowed the circumstances of your life to dim your light, listening to the voices of reason and of fear. "I'm too old," "I already tried and failed," and "It's too late." But listen closely: there is another voice whispering to you, even as it recognizes all your inadequacies and shortcomings, daring you to take the risk of sharing all that you really are with the world.

"When I was young, I faced sexual harassment in my workplace but kept my mouth shut because I was afraid of getting fired," says Lucille, one of our research participants, now 66.

"Then, when I advanced to a new position and was no longer in personal jeopardy, I got caught up in advancing my career. Even though I knew that the problem had not gone away for others, I told myself I'd get back around to it 'when I had more clout.'

"In my forties, when I did have enough clout, I was too exhausted to take on anything else. In my fifties, I began reaping the rewards of all my years of hard work, and the last thing I wanted to do was to rock the boat. 'It's the next generation's turn to fight the good fight,' I told myself.

"Then in my sixties, I retired. Somebody asked me to mentor her niece, Linda, a young woman of great promise. As fate would have it, Linda reluctantly admitted to me that she was being sexually harassed at work but made me promise not to tell. Then and there, I realized that it is possible to let one's whole life pass, never once finding the perfect opportunity to say 'It's me. It's now.' Well guess what! It is me and it is now!" Lucille became active, addressing sexual harassment in her industry, and giving voice to the issue that had lurked in the shadows all her life.

Lucille came to realize that her personal road to meaning entailed standing up to an industry dominated by men, many of whom would just as soon she continued to keep her mouth shut. Thinking about Linda, she now realizes. "Isn't it time we spoke up, becoming dangerous to the status quo?"

For all of us who have come to hold the conviction that our lives, even the difficult and shameful parts, can be turned to the good, here's our salute to you:

A SALUTE TO DANGEROUS WOMEN

A salute to all those who have the courage to test their beliefs against injustice.

A salute to all those who have the strength to challenge others when you see wrongs in the world.

A salute to all those willing to relinquish your quest for peace when you are called into discomfort and sacrifice.

A salute to all those who trust that even as you wrestle with impossible issues, often it is in the struggle, itself, where you will find meaning.

85
Livingness

———●———

I still want to do my work. I still want to do my livingness.
SCULPTOR LOUISE NEVELSON, THEN IN HER LATE 80S

"When my husband died, I was left with enough money to cruise away the rest of my days comfortably ensconced on the deck chair of a luxury liner," says Miranda. "On my very first cruise, I decided to join in on a group tour of one of the ports. While our attention was being directed towards historical landmarks and museums, I kept catching glimpses of children living in hunger and poverty just steps away. I couldn't get over the contrast and to tell you the truth, when I thought of all the food that I had personally consumed that day alone, I felt more than a little guilty." When Miranda returned home, she wanted to do something about what she had seen.

"But who was I to take on such a big undertaking?" she asked herself. "I'm just one person!" Then a friend shared with her a quote by Zora Neal Hurston. "Mama exhorted her children at every opportunity to 'jump at de sun.' We might not land on the sun, but at least we would get off the ground."

When Miranda attended one of our research groups, she was in the midst of considering whether she should get involved in an existing charity that brought humanitarian aid to the children of the region, or start a foundation of her own.

"The thing is to be willing to feel your inadequacy and the fear, and do it anyway," says Miranda.

Miranda's learning reminded us of one of our favorite stories. When Carol was pursuing her master of theological studies at Vanderbilt, Don Beisswinger, one of her favorite professors, announced plans to retire.

"What are you going to do with your life now?" one of the younger graduate students in the class inquired.

"I'm going to work and live among the homeless in Atlanta, ministering to their needs," Don replied.

"You can't be serious!" said the student. "How much can you hope to accomplish given the time you have left?"

Don sighed:

"I know that my task is huge, and time too short. But what you don't understand is that what I'm doing is just the first part of a two-hundred-year plan."

86
What the World Needs

———•———

Don't ask what the world needs.
Ask yourself what makes you come alive.
Then go do it. Because what the world needs
is more people who have come alive.
HOWARD THURMAN

87
Through a Child's Eyes

━━●━━

We must not only give what we have;
we must also give what we are.
DESIRE MERCIER

D otty reports that when she hit 70, she began worrying
about the size and nature of her legacy. Living close to her
daughter, she had her hands full caring for her three
grandchildren after school while her daughter worked. A woman of
modest means, she thought she should do volunteer work, write a
book, become a mentor to adults who could not read, something
memorable to give her life meaning. But spending so much time
with her grandchildren, where was she going to find the time to
make a contribution worthy of her?

"Then it occurred to me that when you ask people 'who was
the most important influence on your life?' they often mention a
grandparent. And what they remember are simple things, like the
shape of their grandmother's hands. The songs they sang together."

Dotty decided to relax and enjoy the time with her
grandchildren, trusting that she was doing exactly what she was
meant to do.

Thinking about Dotty's story, and after spending the afternoon
with her own granddaughter, Niki, Jimmy wrote the following poem.

THROUGH A CHILD'S EYES

Have you ever seen yourself through a child's eyes?
She doesn't ask you how old you are
*   or whether you are important.*
She only cares that you are old enough to read her favorite book
*   to her.*
She only cares that you color with her in her coloring books.
She only cares that you know how to cut out paper dolls.
She only cares that you share her Oreo cookies and milk.
A child doesn't ask how successful you have been
*   or whether you've accomplished all your goals.*
She only cares that you play dress up with her,
*   never knowing that the costumes that make you laugh together*
*   were, until then, long-forgotten heirlooms stored in the closet!*
The child only cares that you giggle over the least little thing,
*   like she does.*
For an afternoon with a child
*   brings out all the wonderful things that we have forgotten,*
*   sweeping us up into the innocent world of wonder*
*   where everything you can imagine is possible!*

Many of us miss our opportunity to imagine the possibilities, because we are so concerned about finding a grand enough cause or great enough purpose worthy of us. While we are anxiously seeking the meaning of our lives through works and deeds, we forget to ask what God is asking of us, right here, right now.

You don't need to know whether you are fulfilling your potential, making a significant contribution, leaving your mark on generations to come. It will always have been enough to do even small things, as long as they are done with great love.

88
Chronological Order

———◦———

When Jill went to visit her mother at the assisted living center, her mother asked if she would mind waiting downstairs in the lobby for a half an hour. "I'm working on the nose on my self-portrait, and I don't want the paint to dry," Dorothy, 91, replied.

"My mother's enthusiasm got me thinking," Jill shared at one of our workshops. "I was in a period of more or less treading water in my own life, having fallen into a comfortable routine that kept me busy but didn't really feed my soul. In fact, I found myself feeling jealous of my mother's passion, realizing that her dreams, even at 91, had so much more life in them than my own."

Then and there, Jill decided that she needed a new dream. "I couldn't think of anything I really wanted to do. But then I ran into a friend who told me that she was reading every Pulitzer Prize-winning novel chronologically. It sounded like such an exciting challenge, I could hardly wait to begin!"

"Every man has his Bethlehem where new possibilities and hopes are born," writes author Sam Keen. "At such times the tyranny of the past and the terror of the future give way before a new time of open possibility—the vibrant present."

89
The Storyteller

———⬤———

very life has a story to tell: some message, some learning, some inherent beauty that captures wisdom to pass to on to generations to come. The story may take the form of words, the yearning you feel to write a poem, a letter, a journal entry, a book. Or it may be a photograph, a painting or a song.

What is this urge to record for posterity? Joan Erikson observes that "a deep need appears to exist in humankind to grasp and give auditory, visual, kinesthetic, and plastic form to sensations and ideas that, unless grounded in the senses and stored in long-term memory, become evanescent; an expression, no doubt, of our constant struggle to deal with loss and change. Memory fades and the need is urgent to communicate with, be recognized by, and record for posterity—to make permanent these deeply sensed experiences."

It is told that when Rabbi Israel Baal Shem-Tov saw misfortune threatening his people, he went to a special place in the forest to meditate. He would light a fire, say a certain prayer, and intercede with God.

When his disciple, the Magid of Mezritch, was faced with the same task for his generation, he would go to the same place and say, "Master of the Universe, Listen! I do not know how to light the fire, but I am still able to say the prayer."

Still later, Rabbi Moshe-Leib of Sasov went to the forest to help his people, saying, "I do not know how to light the fire. I do not know the prayer, but I know the place and that must be sufficient."

Then it was up to Rabbi Israel of Rizhyn to appeal to God. Sitting in his chair, his head in his hands, he said, "I am unable to light the fire. I do not know the prayer. I cannot even find the place in the forest. All I can do is tell the story."

90
For the Generations

———⬛●⬛———

Recently, we were invited to an art opening at a retirement center. On the walls were photographs, oil paintings and sketches. The highlight of the grand opening was a poetry reading with Mabel, Sylvia and Carl—in their 80s and up—sharing their beautifully crafted words of wisdom, inspiration, wry humor and beauty.

And so it is that long after the urge for material goods is satisfied, the urge for fame irrelevant, an afterthought or even a bother, there remains the desire to create.

- Michelangelo was sculpting until the week before he died at 89.
- Louise Nevelson started sculpting when nearly 50 and continued into her late 80s.
- Production designer Henry Bumstead, 89, was part of the winning team that won an Oscar for "Million Dollar Baby."
- Jimmy Laura Smull and Carol Orsborn, at sixty-something and fifty-something, are writing this book.
- What is the story that is uniquely yours to tell?

CREATING A LEGACY

THE FEAR
*That if I haven't achieved something tangible and significant,
I will have fallen short of my life purpose.*

THE TRUTH
*Your true legacy is the summation
of your whole life experience, successes and shortcomings,
culminating with what matters most:
what and how well you've learned to love.*

Meaning

THE SILVER PEARL

Sometimes into the midst of our optimism,
   darkness descends.
We find ourselves wondering what life is about
   and whether we will truly ever find meaning.

Adding to the pain, we question what is wrong with us for even asking,
      and whether we have the right to despair,
      as if shivering naked before the mystery is our choice
      and suffering, optional.

The truth is that for those of us who seek meaning,
      there is no other way than to follow the path that leads
      into the shadows,
      understanding that life sometimes seems to ask more of us
      than we think we have to give.

Give it anyway, and stripped to your essence,
      you will discover that all along,
      meaning was never something for you to find—
      but rather, something for you to make.

91
Youthful Illusion

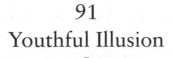

When we are young, we think that the purpose of life is to be happy. As long as we are thinking smarter, trying harder and working longer, we believe that it is entirely in our power to achieve our goals, and that it is in the achievement of our goals that we will find meaning.

The truth is: sooner or later, something always goes wrong. We suffer losses. We experience sadness. We become disappointed. And ultimately, we find ourselves questioning the meaning of our lives.

As long as we are attempting to hold onto the illusions of our youth, we are bound to confuse this yearning for meaning with the quest for power, as if the answer will be found in the next achievement.

But meaning bursts open the narrow bands of human desire and forces us to embrace the full range of the human potential. Righteous indignation! Bittersweet sadness! Forgiveness! Despair!

These are potent emotions, capable of exposing the core question that every human being must ask of herself if she hopes to come to terms with the meaning of life: *Is this a loving universe—or not?*

Whatever it costs you, the only way out of this abyss is to somehow find a "yes," leaping for affirmation as if it were a rope thrown to you in the depths of the mystery.

For regardless of how great the circumstantial evidence to the contrary, there is no alternative but to take the leap of faith that life has purpose, that self-sacrifice has meaning, and that the divine calls to us for some greater reason than we may ever be able to fully grasp.

This is the transformed experience of being alive. It causes us to transcend self-interest in order to take the risk of believing that it is worthwhile to love others, to make sacrifices for others, even knowing that in doing so, one becomes vulnerable, exposes oneself to pain and the potential for disappointment. This, in fact, is the very essence of what we are experiencing when many among us refer to God.

By leaping to "yes," you imbue your life with the possibility of meaning, understanding that all along, meaning was never something you would find but rather, something that, with God's help, you accomplish.

92
Reunion

———●———

Perhaps a stable order can only be established on earth
if man always remains acutely conscious
that his condition is that of a traveler.
GABRIEL MARCEL

When he was in his sixties, the scholar Sam Keen revisited the spiritual autobiography of his life, *To a Dancing God*, written while in his forties. In the twenty years that passed, Sam learned many more of life's lessons. There was joy, but there were tragedies, as well, most notably the demise of his marriage, taking down with it many of the illusions of youth. Through it all, he remained haunted by questions: *"Why am I restless? Anxious? Why am I so hollowed out by longing and etched by the acid of loneliness?"*

But revisiting these questions after two decades had passed, Sam noticed a difference. At the age of 60, he no longer felt that the questions represented a problem to be solved. Rather, it was the very act of asking the questions that comprised the unfolding of the journey, itself.

Right now, it is possible that you, too, have questions that cannot be easily resolved "but dare not be forgotten." You may fear that you have been abandoned, that pieces of you have been dealt away in failure or shame. In the depths of the dark night, well may you yearn for wholeness.

It is the same feeling as when you are homesick. Separated from home and from those who love you, yearning settles heavily upon your heart. Part of you has been left behind. You ache for reconciliation.

But consider this: when you are homesick, you can feel such acute pain only because you know what home means, and what it is to be loved. Just as homesickness points to your experience of a real home, real love, so does yearning contain the memory of what has also already truly been yours. It is your unrest, itself, that proclaims the truth that wholeness of spirit is real and possible. You can feel this way only because you know what connection to the divine means, and what it is to be loved by God. In truth, it is as the mystics teach: You would not yearn if you had not already been found.

93
The Route to Meaning

———◦———

In *Mourning and Mitzvah*, Anne Brener describes a terrifying period in her life in which she felt very much alone. She had just lost her mother to suicide when just three months later, her sister, her only sibling, was killed in a car accident. Anne's response was to try to take her mind off her losses by putting herself into challenging and risky situations.

One day, while swimming in the Umpqua River in southern Oregon, Anne got caught in a dangerous current. "Struggling to cross the river, my energy ran out. I realized that I was going to drown. I thought sadly of my beloved father, whose losses had already been so great. I took a deep breath and let the current carry me downstream."

Ironically, when Anne surrendered to the current, her body relaxed. She was able to catch her breath and regain strength. When the river narrowed, she found herself able to swim across the rapids to the shore. "What began with a deep breath of surrender had saved my life."

For Anne, the encounter with the river initiated a lengthy period of healing, in which the separation she had felt from those whom she had loved and lost began to feel less absolute. Now, years later, spirituality has been incorporated into the fabric of her life. Anne is guiding others through the sometimes frightening "but always interesting" currents of life towards meaning.

Swept down the rapids of your own life, when all seems lost, your only recourse is to relinquish your powerlessness and put your trust in forces greater than yourself. They are working invisibly on your behalf every moment of your life.

As writer Dorothy Lessing notes:

Almost all people "have strange imaginings. The strangest of these is a belief that they can progress only by improvement." We think it is up to us, to our own fretful efforts and struggles towards mastery. But Dorothy continues: "Those who understand will realize that we are much more in need of stripping off than adding on."

94
The Healthy Spirituality Test

———◦●◦———

Traditionally, religion has been the arbiter of meaning in our lives. Follow the rules, believe the stories, and you will be rewarded with the knowledge of how the world works and your secure place within it.

However, simply by asking questions, many of us have found ourselves exiled from the religions of our childhood. Our search for answers has taken us beyond the boundaries of dogma and belief, navigating new spiritual terrain without the aid of a familiar map to point the way.

Recently, Jimmy had a conversation with her son, Jack, a grown man with a family of his own. Jack reminded Jimmy that when he was still in school, she had tried to find a non–denominational church for the two to attend, a far cry from the hellfire and brimstone church within which she had been raised. But having raised Jack to think for himself, he had already begun researching religion and spirituality on his own. In fact, one day, he came home from the library with a stack of books to write a book report. When Jimmy asked him what it was about, he said "Zoroastrianism!" Jimmy had to go to the dictionary and look it up. Soon after, he became enthralled with the book *Siddhartha* by Herman Hesse. The two spent many long happy hours engaged in discussions about eastern and western philosophy, spirituality and religion.

During a recent phone call, Jimmy asked Jack where he was in his beliefs now. She could not help but feel a quiet joy when he told her that he is on a search for what he calls an unseen universal order. Is it physics, astrophysics, intuition, spirituality or a combination? He wasn't ready to give it a name. Whatever he ends up calling it, Jimmy was pleased that her son had retained the sense that we are not alone in a chaotic universe—but rather, that there is some sense to existence.

Even under the best of circumstances, moving forward onto new spiritual terrain without a tried and true map can be justifiably anxiety producing. But even if your quest for meaning brings you to unfamiliar territory, there are ways to expand your comfort level.

In *The Mythic Path*, Drs. Krippner and Feinstein provide a simple test that can be adapted easily to provide guidance. Simply ask yourself:

Does your spirituality "usher you toward more fulfilling relationships, more rewarding social activities, greater social support, a present-centered absorption in the flow of life, physical fitness, and enough rest and personal solitude, all of which are also associated with happiness?"

Answer this in the affirmative and you can trust that you have found a spiritual path worth exploring. You can keep the best of your religious upbringing, discard what no longer serves you and experiment with new, creative options—trusting that after all you've been through, you can sort out the toxic from the life-giving. If you make a mistake, you can correct quickly and move on. In time, you will have a portfolio of beliefs and practices that support your authentic self: a place you will be free to call your true spiritual home.

95
Seraphim

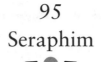

Many years ago, between Linn's first and second rounds of chemotherapy for breast cancer, it suddenly became very important to her to get Dan and the kids to help her paint the kitchen. Given the circumstances, they would most probably have done anything for her. But what Linn wanted most was a painted kitchen. Tan. So there they were, the four of them wearing old baseball caps, splattered with paint, working to the beat of the Beatles blasting from the boom box.

Toward the end of the weekend, they were standing back admiring their work when Linn burst into tears. Not knowing what was wrong, her family huddled around her until she could finally choke out what was going on.

You see, Linn had been overwhelmed by her love for them. In truth, Linn's love was so strong, she felt like she was burning up inside. She was like the Seraphim in Jewish midrash, angels in attendance to God whose only job is to recite "Holy, Holy, Holy." The thing is, as the tradition goes, the passion of their emotion is so great, the angels can only get partway through the first holy before burning up with love.

96
Final Analysis

———◆———

By now, it is becoming obvious that seeking meaning in life is
not only about finding simple happiness or inner peace or
even an unshakable stability. While it is true that there are
moments when we can know that our souls are at home in the
world, when the universe seems luminous with never-ending peace
and joy, it is also true that so long as you are fully alive, there can be
no safety in your choices. What then? In the words of a much-
beloved poem: "Give the world the best you've got anyway." Here
is an excerpt from the poem.

What you spend years building, someone may destroy overnight;
  Build anyway.
If you find serenity and happiness, they may be jealous;
  Be happy anyway.
The good you do today, people will often forget tomorrow;
  Do good anyway.
Give the world the best you have, and it may never be enough;
  Give the world the best you've got anyway.

97
Full Bloom

In the midst of her doctoral coursework, Jimmy blocked out time alone for a writing retreat. The assignment was to write an essay titled: "The Experience of Disillusionment with One's Personal Mythology." Before Jimmy could even open her first resource book, she found herself instead rushing to put pen to paper as for the first time in her life. A poem poured out of her. She recognized in this poem a message from the depths of her heart, letting her know that she had, at last, integrated all the various aspects of her life into a whole.

In *Wisdom and the Senses*, Joan Erikson refers to this state as "the final existential identity," an inner core that represents an integration of past, present, and future. This is the state that we refer to as the Silver Pearl.

"The cycle of life itself, especially as elders consistently seek to integrate its many aspects, unfolds a supreme wonder. All sentient things come into being, integrate, develop, become, fulfill an appointed role, and die, to be returned to the earth. The whole earth, the planet, the cosmos, is in a state of constant change. We are all and with everything, involved in a process," writes Joan.

In writing her poem, Jimmy engaged in this process of integration by putting the pain of her memories into perspective, acknowledging the good and incorporating everything into a whole, going forth with a new sense of meaning. This is Jimmy's poem.

Life is a fabric, which is woven from beginning to end
A tree's life is similar—and branches should blend

Life must honor its roots from which it grows
Just as the tree takes its lumps—only the strong ones will last

Life has a story to tell if anyone will listen
Just as the tree reveals its story on branches that glisten

The fabric of life woven so tight
Looks back and says it doesn't matter who's wrong or who's right

The tree is in full bloom for all to gaze
Knows that it all comes together in mysterious ways

98
Gates of Heaven

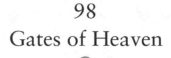

The woman stood before the angel, so many tears streaming down her face that she could not read the letters on the gate. While she had always tried to live a good life, the sorrow that consumed her sent a shiver of fear down her spine. At last, trembling in fear, she managed to ask the angel her question.

"Am I at the gates of heaven—or of hell?" she whispered.

"Tell me first," the angel replied. "Why are you crying?"

The woman stopped to think, and into her mind flooded images of all that she had left behind. Not only her husband, with whom she'd spent fifty years, but the memories of a lifetime full of simple joys and unavoidable losses. Her parents, young and full of life, pushing her proudly through the streets of their neighborhood in a brand-new stroller. Childhood friends building castles in the sand, blown to dust by the churning wheels of time. High-school proms, college, their wedding night. Then there were her babies— first steps, names in school programs, graduations, leaving home for the last time, children no more. Along the way, there were new houses, new cities, new jobs—some left out of choice, some not. There was falling down and starting over again. And then, too, there was the gradual loss of her physical vitality and ultimately her own death.

Witnessing all, the angel finally replied, "Only one who has loved so greatly can feel such great pain. You stand here before the gates to heaven or to hell. And so it is before I answer your question that you must answer one for me. Have you been blessed or have you been cursed?"

So surprised was she by the angel's words that her eyes suddenly cleared. Had she been blessed or had she been cursed? For many moments, she reviewed her life, pondering the angel's question.

"If it was a curse," she finally declared, "I would give none of it back."

With that, her fear departed, leaving in its wake only the bittersweet song of her love. Had she given her life her very best? She no longer needed to read the word above the gate to determine her destiny. The angel took her hand and together they walked through the celestial gates.

99
Sunset

Once upon a time, the story goes, a seeker heard word of a spiritual master who had spent many years meditating at the peak of a mountain about the meaning of life.

With great intention, the seeker left her home and traversed many miles to reach the base of the mountain. Then, with even greater effort, she ascended to the top.

Once there, so exhausted by her journey that she could only muster energy enough to crawl on hands and knees, she finally made it to the feet of the master.

"Master, master," she cried, rousing him from his meditation.

"You have contemplated the meaning of life for so many years, and I have come so far and worked so hard to find out the secret from you. Please, master, tell me: what is the meaning of life?"

The master regarded the seeker intently, took a deep breath, and replied:

"It's the sunset."

"The sunset?" the seeker responded.

There was a long pause and at last, the master spoke again.

"You mean, it's not the sunset?"

100
In Retrospect

———•———

One day in retrospect the years of struggle
will strike you as the most beautiful.
SIGMUND FREUD

MEANING

THE FEAR
*There's something wrong with you
if you feel the need to ask the big questions about life.*

THE TRUTH
*You can yearn for answers about meaning
only because you sense a connection to the divine
that is already yours.*

———————————

APPENDIX

The Theoretical Foundation
of the Silver Pearl

In the 1950s, anthropologist Margaret Mead delivered a memorable lecture about the role of the postmenopausal red-tailed deer. Margaret explained that in their advanced years, when all the old bucks had been killed off in skirmishes, the females became the oldest survivors.

"In time of drought, these old does could remember where once, long ago, under similar circumstances, water sources had been found. When spring came late, they recalled sunny slopes where the snows melted early. They knew how to find shelter, places where blizzards could be waited out. Under such circumstances, they took over the leadership of the herd."

Seated in the audience of Margaret's lecture was the young Joan Erikson, wife of the champion of developmental psychology, Erik Erikson, and an intellectual and artist, in her own right. Years later, Joan, well into her 80s, revisited Margaret's story about the red-tailed deer to deliver a message that goes straight to the heart of the women of our generation. In an age when society still tends to think of aging as a problem, undervaluing, marginalizing or even dismissing older women outright, Joan recognized the contribution of extended time and experience to the achievement of psychological and spiritual growth.

DEFYING CLASSICAL THEORY

The celebration of the notion of lifelong development stands in defiance of the classical developmental theorists. These include scholars such as Jean Piaget, who correlated the stages of psychological and spiritual growth with the stages of physical development. Piaget, concentrating his attention on intellectual growth, privileged the importance of childhood over later periods of our lives. In the limited view of these early life theorists, those of us at midlife and beyond are perceived as primarily passive recipients of our early childhood influences—no longer creators of our destinies.

Erik Erikson, Joan's husband, was among those who questioned this premise, stretching the boundaries of developmental theory to cover the entire lifespan of the individual. However, even Erik's notion of eight life stages cast the mature individual in a largely passive role. On Erik's model of the life cycle, the fulfillment of one's potential culminated with stepping out of the way to allow the next generation to come into its own. Ironically, as Erik and Joan aged, he was quickly revising his stages as he went. In his last book, a collaboration with Joan, he added a ninth stage to acknowledge that their own creative powers paid witness to the novel notion that psychological and spiritual development could grow in strength and vitality throughout one's life. In her follow-up book, Wisdom and the Senses, written well into her eighties, Joan summarized their revolutionary late-in-life realization: "The whole earth, the planet, the cosmos, is in a state of constant change. We are all and with everything, involved in a process."

The revolutionary aspect of this revised notion of lifelong psychological and spiritual growth is that, unlike physical development, the older you become, the more possible is it for you to achieve your fullest potential. That lifelong psychological and spiritual advancement is possible is supported by our original research, including in-depth conversations with over one hundred women who have achieved mastery in one or more areas of their lives.

CULTURAL MYTHOLOGY

We find a particularly useful model for lifelong growth in cultural mythology, an illuminating theory about human development, introduced to us by Drs. Stanley Krippner and David Feinstein. From the perspective of the cultural mythologists, the child is born into an original worldview—or, as they refer to it, "myth"—that functions in such a way as to give that child's life meaning. In healthy development, when new information that differs from the original worldview is introduced into the child's life, the individual either modifies or replaces the old myth. The old myth must be acknowledged as being outdated or dysfunctional in order for the person to advance and grow.

The fulfillment of this potential is not a free and easy ascent. For women, the normal stages of development are routinely delayed, halted or skipped entirely as over and over again, we are asked to deny our own sense of life and the ability to think for ourselves in deference to other people's worldviews. Even as adults, the imposition continues. Every day, the women of our generation are confronted by stereotypes of aging and dire warnings about our futures. The tendency to buy into outdated notions in present time stems from beliefs that we were taught at an earlier age: that if we disagree with what the authorities are teaching us, it is we who are crazy, bad or doomed.

Key to advancing from this stage of development is the recognition, often painful, of what has been missed. We need to dig through layers upon layers in search of the authentic self buried beneath. In Dr. Krippner's words: the goal is to target old patterns of belief "that are dysfunctional, even if long held and consistently confirmed by the logic of long-standing beliefs. To the degree you are able to bring about constructive changes in such fundamental perspectives, positive shifts in your life will tend to follow."

There are many emotions, as well as behaviors, that can trigger the awareness that there is inner work to be done. Some of the more common indicators that may be showing up in your life include the consistent inability to make a decision, the nagging sense that you are perceived by others differently than how you feel inside, persistent self-neglect of your physical or emotional needs, free-floating anxiety, and so on. At last, you can confront these negative messages and self-defeating patterns head-on, not as a problem to feel bad about, but as providing important clues in regards to where to begin.

When you read through the following list of hidden messages, you may encounter old messages, pains and memories you thought you'd already left behind. But remember, the moment you make a conscious effort to turn towards rather than away from the pain, you begin making up lost ground. Without doing anything more than feel, you will find yourself spontaneously progressing towards the resolution you seek.

Earlier, you took Your Silver Pearl Wisdom Inventory, assessing your stage of development in regards to the top ten issues cited by women in our study. If you gave a Stage One response in any of these ten areas, here is a limiting message from your past that was embedded in your answer.

1. Preparing for the Future: When I see myself as worrying justifiably about what lies ahead... *The Hidden Message is: The future is a dangerous place.*

2. Ambition: When I see myself as falling short of expectations set for me... *The Hidden Message is: It is disloyal to put your own desires before the needs and expectations of others.*

3. Love and Relationships: When I see myself as viewing toxic relationships with past, current or potential mates/friends/relatives as pretty much the norm... *The Hidden Message is: You're not worthy of respect. Your needs don't matter.*

4. Parenting Grown Children: When I see myself as viewing my children's success as a reflection of my own self-worth... *The Hidden Message is: Your value as a woman is measured by other people's opinions of the success of your children.*

5. Unfinished Business: When I see myself as unable to do anything about it now... *The Hidden Message is: Don't rock the boat or it will sink you.*

6. Beauty: When I see myself as defining my success in relation to looks... *The Hidden Message is: It is a matter of external judgment as to whether I am beautiful or not.*

7. Health: When I see myself as viewing illness as some kind of shortcoming... *The Hidden Message is: Sickness is a weakness.*

8. Caregiving, Loss and Inevitabilities: When I see myself thinking of decline and death as failure... The Hidden Message is: Dying means "you lose."

9. Creating a Legacy: When I see myself believing that a life must be measured by what is left behind... *The Hidden Message is: You are imperfect the way you are.*

10. Meaning: When I see myself wondering what's wrong with me that I can't just be happy with what I have... *The Hidden Message is: There's something wrong with you if you feel the need to ask the big questions.*

By acknowledging these hidden messages, you will be able to make a conscious choice about whether to keep them or cast them away. If you choose to cast them away, you will initiate the next period of growth in the areas of concern to you.

The targeting of old belief patterns is no simple matter, as one becomes dis-illusioned with that which one had previously taken for granted. The woman in this stage often feels herself to be plunged into a seemingly bottomless pit, her old status quo crumbling beneath her feet as she frantically clutches at empty air looking for something solid to grab onto. The old myth is falling apart—but the new, healthier worldview has not yet come into view.

RITES OF PASSAGE

In many respects, this vulnerable period bears similarities to a rite of passage. In the classic ritual, the initiate is separated from the familiarity of the everyday life of the tribe and put through a series of trials. In the end, transformed by the experience, the initiate re-enters the tribe with the new stature of an adult, having gained valuable skills and insights.

Contemporary anthropologists suggest that individuals undergoing transitions at any stage of their lives go through a similar initiatory sequence, often experienced inwardly as an altered emotional state. For many of the women we interviewed, the advance from Stage One to Stage Two was initiated by some kind of separation from the context within which they had come to know themselves, such as moving to a new city, divorce, career or job transitions, death of a family member, illness or any of the definitive events that take us out of the familiar routines of our lives. Ironically, happy occasions, too, such as the marriage of a child, can trigger such a response.

At the same time the old conceptions are passing away, signs of new beliefs and behaviors formed in reaction to them begin to emerge. For example, tired of trying to live up to other people's expectations about beauty, one of our research participants, Samantha, decided to cut her long hair into a crew cut, letting what was left of her mane go a natural gray. Another participant, Elizabeth, frustrated over being asked to head up the hospitality committee, once again simply stopped going to church, having been denied a seat of power on the board.

Of the possible self-protective reactions you could have, the most efficient place from which to advance beyond Stage Two is from a state of active rebellion. To rebel is to reject energetically the limiting belief system in which you were raised. Getting in touch with and expressing this rebellious energy may be a stretch for you, but it is not a particularly exceptional state in the scheme of things. Rebellion, after all, is the stage of life that is normally associated with adolescence. Never mind that many of our co-researchers were sixty and over. The miracle is that at any age, we can more than make up for lost time. But as healthy a developmental stage as this may be, it is possible to get stuck, even here.

GETTING UNSTUCK

Ironically, being stuck in rebellion can look like productive, creative energy. It may, in fact, be the stage of choice for many high performing individuals, such as artists, businesswomen and professionals. However, the irony is that you may look to all the world as if you have somehow beaten the game to win your freedom, when all you've really done is replace one set of programming with another. As long as your beliefs and actions are primarily reactions to the worldview to which you were born, even your rebellious choices are limited, locking you into a relationship with destructive beliefs, rather than setting you free. As much as you've accomplished, as long as you are in Stage Two, you will simply not be as powerful as you have always suspected you could be. You will know that you are back on track to making real progress when you become aware of what others have done to you, and of what your own self-protective reactions have done to yourself.

As unpleasant as it may be, disillusionment is natural and inevitable. If you try to skip this stage, continuing to hang on to the past, you will repeatedly find yourself in situations that damage you. You will feel restricted and burdened. Through the healthy process of disillusionment, you acknowledge the old views of the world and self as being outdated or dysfunctional so that you can glimpse and nurture a more authentic, healthier view of the world and yourself.

In the words of Bill Bridges, who writes about disillusionment in his book *Transitions*: "One must surrender and give into the emptiness and stop struggling to escape it. Chaos is not a mess. Rather it is the primal state of pure energy to which the person returns for every true new beginning. It is only from the perspective of the old form that chaos looks fearful. From any other perspective, it looks like life itself, as yet unshaped by purpose and identification."

GOING FOR THE SILVER PEARL

Again, while disillusionment is not something most of us eagerly seek in our lives, it does inevitably herald a new period of growth. Out of the chaos of transition emerges the third and final phase of development that we symbolize with the silver pearl. During this culminating stage, the essential task is to move beyond the victimization of the first stage and the rebellion and reactivity of the second. The hallmark of the authentic life that arises is integrity: an embrace of opposing tensions—the sum of which constitutes a whole greater than any of the parts. The authenticity of the silver pearl is real and unshakable, specifically because it does not leave anything out. It resolves everything that has come before to be fresh and appropriate in the present moment. This, in fact, is the ultimate goal of the developmental progression: not the simplicity or easy gratification of the wholesale annihilation of our pasts, but the thoughtful, gentle melding together of something authentic and unshakable. In Stage Three, we have the opportunity to complete the unfinished work of our earlier life stages—regardless of whatever age we happen to be now.

Each of the women in our study, all of whom are actively engaged in the reclamation of their authentic selves, expressed in her own special way the profound joy and satisfaction that came from the reclamation of authenticity. We may speak of it as happiness, but the experience of authenticity is far more complex—and the pay-off far richer. Of course, we want to feel good, to feel more secure about the future, to believe ourselves to be doing right by our declining parents and grown children, not to mention being loved, healthy and successful. Having worked so hard to reclaim a worldview that offers the possibility of attaining our own, rather than somebody else's dream, we are more likely to reach these exalted states on a more consistent basis. When we do, we have no doubts that the hard work has paid off and that we are, indeed, fulfilling our human potential. But what catches us by surprise is that even when we are in pain—at those difficult times when we find ourselves struggling with doubts, anger, sadness or any of the other darker tones on the emotional scale—we still think the path we've chosen away from both imposed and reactive beliefs and behaviors and toward our authentic lives is a journey well worth taking.

RESOURCE GUIDE

Achterberg, Jeanne. *Woman as Healer.* Boston: Shambhala, 1990. *An historical background on women in the healing arts.*

Artress, Lauren. *Walking A Sacred Path: Rediscovering the Labyrinth as a Spiritual Tool.* New York: Riverhead Books, 1995. *Artress shows us how a walking meditation can be a powerful tool for transformation.*

Beattie, Melody. *The Language of Letting Go: Daily Meditations for Codependents.* New York: HarperCollins, 1990. *These daily meditations give voice to the thoughts and feelings common to men and women in recovery.*

Boland, Karen. *Woman Awareness (Audio).* Warren, MI: Master Mind Publishing Company, 1983. *Boland teaches us how to break down internal structures that are keeping us away from our highest good.*

Boland, Karen. *Life Never Ends (Audio).* Warren, MI: Master Mind Publishing Company, 1986. *New conditioning toward death helps us to accept death fearlessly, as a simple transition.*

Borysenko, Joan. *Pocketful of Miracles: Prayers, Meditations and Affirmations to Nurture Your Spirit Every Day of the Year.* New York: Warner Books, 1997. *A thoughtful and useful guide to everyday life.*

Breathnach, Sarah Ban. *Simple Abundance: a Daybook of Comfort and Joy.* New York: Warner, 1995. *This Daily Reader shows you how your daily life can be an expression of your authentic self.*

*Bridges, William. *Transitions: Making Sense of Life's Changes.* New York: Perseus Book Publishing, 1980. *A helpful book that translates anthropological studies of ritual theory into layperson's terms.*

Cameron, Julia. *The Artist's Way: A Spiritual Path to Higher Creativity.* New York: Jeremy P. Tarcher/Putnam, 1992. *A sourcebook for the relationship between creativity and human potential.*

Citron, Sterna. *Why the Baal Shem Tov Laughed: Fifty-Two Stories about Our Great Chasidic Rabbis.* NJ: Jason Aronson, 1993. *A fine, inspiring collection of stories from the Jewish tradition.*

Dossey, Larry. *Healing Words: The Power of Prayer and The Practice of Medicine.* San Francisco: Harper, 1993. *Dossey shows us how prayer, health and healing are integrated.*

Dreamer, Oriah Mountain. *The Invitation.* San Francisco: Harper, 1999. *This book challenges us to be open to love and life.*

*Erikson, E. *Identity: Youth and Crisis.* New York: W. W. Norton & Company, 1968. *Erikson suggests that it is vital for young people to decide how our evolution will take place by confirming or disavowing societal precepts based upon what is good for society.*

Erikson, Joan. *Wisdom and the Senses.* New York: W. W. Norton & Company, 1988. *Shows how personal growth can continue throughout our lives.*

*Feinstein, D., & Krippner, S. *Personal Mythology: The Psychology of Your Evolving Self.* Los Angeles, CA: Jeremy P. Tarcher, 1988. *The authors challenge you to become aware of the mythology under which you are living, and then, to confront it and master it.*

*Feinstein, D., & Krippner, S. *The Mythic Path: Discovering the Guiding Stories of Your Past-Creating a Vision for Your Future.* New York: Putnam/Jeremy P. Tarcher, 1997. *Through ritual, dreams and imagination the authors help you become less bound by the mythologies of childhood and culture.*

Hicks, J., & E. *A New Beginning I.* San Antonio, TX: Abraham-Hicks Publications, 1988. *This little book insists that we are here on earth to experience joy, and everything else we need will follow.*

Houston, Jean. *A Mythic Life: Learning to Live Our Greater Story.* San Francisco: Harper, 1996. *Drawing from real life, Houston reveals how to discover our real potential.*

James, Jennifer. *Success Is the Quality of Your Journey.* New York: Newmarket Press, 1983. *James reminds us that making the right choices in our lives can enhance the quality of our lives.*

James, William. *The Varieties of Religious Experience*. Boston: Mentor Books, 1902. *Description of various types of spiritual awakenings.*

Keen, Sam. *To a Dancing God: Notes of a Spiritual Traveler*. San Francisco: Harper, 1990. *Spiritual autobiography of a theologian and philosopher.*

*Kimble, Melvin et al. *Aging, Spirituality and Religion: A Handbook*. Minneapolis: Fortress Press, 1995. *Scholars from a variety of disciplines contribute to this standard reference work in the emerging interdisciplinary field of aging, religion and spirituality.*

Kornfield, Jack. *A Path with Heart: A Guide Through the Perils and Promises of Spiritual Life*. New York: Bantam, 1993. *Kornfield presents practical techniques and guided meditations, and speaks to the concerns of many modern spiritual seekers.*

Kubler-Ross, Elisabeth. *The Wheel of Life: A Memoir of Living and Dying*. New York: Touchstone, 1997. *The scholar's life story, giving us lessons on how to live well.*

Kuner, S.; Orsborn, C.; Quigley, L.; & Stroup, K. *Speak the Language of Healing: Living with Breast Cancer without Going to War*. Berkeley, CA: Conari Press, 1999. *A new way of thinking about and living with life-threatening illness.*

Lindbergh, Anne Morrow. *Gift from the Sea*. New York: Pantheon Books, 1995. *A simple book of beauty and wisdom that has inspired generations of women as they navigate the various states and stages of life.*

Missildine, W. H. *Your Inner Child of the Past*. New York: Simon & Schuster, 1963. *Missildine leads you toward modifying attitudes resulting from early childhood experiences. One must treat oneself with the approach of a kindly parent.*

Moore, Thomas. *Care of the Soul*. San Francisco: HarperCollins, 1992. *Encourages the reader to look at reality in a more expansive and meaningful way.*

Northrup, C. *Women's Bodies, Women's Wisdom: Creating Physical and Emotional Health and Healing.* New York: Bantam, 1994. *The women's "Bible" of mind-body wellness.*

Orsborn, C. *The Art of Resilience: 100 Paths to Wisdom and Strength in an Uncertain World.* New York: Three Rivers, 1997. *The author provides guidance to help the reader rebound gracefully and productively against forces beyond one's control.*

Orsborn, C. *Nothing Left Unsaid: Words to Help You and Your Loved Ones through the Hardest Times.* Boston: Conari/Red/Wheel Weiser, 1999. *The author guides the reader through life's most difficult moments.*

Peck, M. Scott. *In Search of Stones: A Pilgrimage of Faith, Reason, and Discovery.* New York: Hyperion, 1995. *By using his own life as an example, the author leads readers to see the truth about themselves, their own lives, and the greater community around them.*

Pert, Candace. "The Chemical Communicators" (pp. 177–193). In *Healing and The Mind* by Bill Moyers. New York: Doubleday, 1993. *Pert's discoveries have led to an understanding of the chemicals that travel between the mind and the body.*

*Piaget, Jean. *The Construction of Reality in the Child.* (M. Cook. Trans.). New York: Basic Books, 1954. *An analysis of the origins of intellectual activity in children.*

*Piaget, Jean. *The Moral Judgment of the Child.* New York: Penguin Books, 1977. *Results of pioneering work on developmental psychology in early childhood.*

Ram Dass. *Still Here: Embracing Aging, Changing, and Dying.* New York: Riverhead Books, 2000. *As always, Ram Dass's inimitable spirit shows how to face change and challenge in our lives.*

Redfield, James. *Celestine Prophecy: An Adventure.* New York: Time Warner, 1993. *Drawn on ancient wisdom, this is a guidebook for recognizing where you are in life. It also infuses your steps toward tomorrow with new energy.*

Sheehy, Gail. *New Passages: Mapping Your Life Across Time.* New York: Random House, 1995. *Sheehy encourages readers to look at the facts, folklore, and fears and take control of their health.*

Sher, Barbara. *I Could Do Anything if I Only Knew What it Was: How to Discover What You Really Want and How to Get It.* New York: Dell Publishing, 1994. *This sourcebook shows how you can recapture "long lost" goals and how to overcome the blocks that inhibit success.*

Sher, Barbara. *It's Only Too Late if You Don't Start Now: How to Create Your Second Life at Any Age.* New York: Dell Publishing, 1998. *Instruction and strategy for creating a "second life."*

*Smull, Jimmy Laura. *Healing Eve: The Woman's Journey from Religious Fundamentalism to Religious Freedom.* Chicago: Ampersand, Inc., 2005. *Moving beyond destructive beliefs about religion to joyful spirituality.*

Thoele, Sue Patton. *The Woman's Book of Courage: Meditations for Empowerment and Peace of Mind.* Berkeley, CA: Red/Wheel Weiser, 1991. *This loving book helps women gain self-esteem and improve relationships.*

Viorst, Judith. *Necessary Losses.* New York: Fawcett Gold Metal, 1986. *Shows the reader how inevitable losses can lead to deeper perspective, maturity and wisdom about life.*

Viscott, David. *Discovering the Love You Have to Give (Audio).* CA: Inner World Audio Publishers, 1985. *Viscott reminds us that the amount of love we have for our ourselves is the amount of love we have for the world.*

Warschaw, Tessa Albert. *Rich is Better.* Garden City, NY: Doubleday, 1985. *The author shows how one can overcome a poverty mentality, which leaves one failing to nurture oneself, feeling guilty, and locked in vacant hope.*

Wilhelm, Richard, and Baynes, Cary F. *The I Ching.* Forward by Carl Jung. Princeton, NJ: Princeton University Press, 1950. *The classic Chinese book of wisdom and divination.*

Wolf, Naomi. *The Beauty Myth: How Images of Beauty Are Used Against Women*. New York: William Morrow, 1991. *Wolf reminds us that women can be punished simply on the basis of their appearance, and women must choose what they will do with their faces and bodies without being influenced by this ideology.*

*Titles marked with an asterisk are recommended for individuals interested in further study of the theoretical underpinnings of *The Silver Pearl* stages. Other books on this list provided inspiration to us as we sought stories, advice and wisdom to describe the Stage Three perspectives we encountered during our studies. We are particularly indebted to Barbara Sher, Joan Erikson, Betty Friedan and Gail Sheehy for their groundbreaking work on the subjects covered in this book.

Looking Forward

For a free self-assessment which allows you to locate yourself on the Silver Pearl model of spiritual and psychological growth on an issue by issue basis, visit our website at www.TheSilverPearl.com. You are also invited to sign up for free inspirational emails and to read an "almost daily blog" inspired by this book.

To e-mail the authors:

Dr. Jimmy Laura Smull—*jlsmull@cox.net*
Dr. Carol Orsborn—*corsborn@aol.com*

ABOUT THE AUTHORS

Jimmy Laura Smull, Ph.D. is a cultural anthropologist and an authority on the subject of adult development. She specializes in helping women identify and break free from destructive childhood ideologies and religious programming so that they can advance psychologically and spiritually. Dr. Smull conducted a "Body, Mind and Spirit" conference for 200 women in New York City in the course of research for her doctorate in philosophy of human science. With the encouragement of professors and colleagues, she published her findings in her first book, *Healing Eve: The Woman's Journey from Religious Fundamentalism to Spiritual Freedom*. In researching The Silver Pearl with Orsborn, Smull applied her model of adult development to the study of women at midlife and beyond who are defying the stereotypes of aging. Her doctorate is from Saybrook Graduate School and Research Center.

Carol Orsborn, Ph.D. first came to national attention when she founded Superwoman's Anonymous, an organization that set the tone early on for her generation of baby boomers. She appeared on "Oprah" and "The Today Show," bringing such revolutionary notions as simplicity and work/life balance to national attention. Orsborn is the author of 15 books related to quality of life. In addition to running www.TheSilverPearl.com, she is a veteran public relations strategist and Co-chair of Fleishman-Hillard's FH Boom, the first initiative by a global PR firm dedicated to helping marketers connect with the boomer consumer. An expert in ritual studies and adult development, Orsborn is a research associate with UCLA. Her doctorate is from Vanderbilt University.